METABOLIC

CONFUSION

HIIT

Unlocking Your Ultimate Fitness

Transformation with Metabolic Confusion HIIT: Workouts, Nutrition, and Expert Insights for Rapid Fat Loss and Lasting Results

Vincent C. Santos

Copyright © 2023 by **Vincent C. Santos**

All rights reserved.

No part of this book may be used or reproduced in any form whatsoever without written permission except in the case of brief quotations in critical articles or reviews.

Printed in the United States of America.

First Edition: **AUGUST 2023**

ABOUT THE AUTHOR:

Vincent C. Santos is an inspiring voice in the realm of fitness and wellness, with a passion for helping individuals harness their full potential through the transformative power of exercise and healthy living. Drawing from his own journey of self-discovery and dedication to holistic health, Vincent brings a unique perspective to his work that resonates deeply with readers seeking to embark on their own fitness adventure.

With a background rooted in sports science and personal training, Vincent C. Santos has spent years honing his expertise in understanding the human body's capabilities and limitations. As the creator of the groundbreaking book "Metabolic Confusion HIIT," he skillfully weaves together his vast knowledge of exercise physiology, nutrition, and mental wellbeing.

Vincent's journey towards creating the "Metabolic Confusion HIIT" method began when he witnessed the transformative impact it had on his own life. Struggling with his fitness goals at one point, he embarked on a quest to find an approach that went beyond the conventional. His deep exploration of various exercise strategies, nutritional insights, and mindful practices led him to develop the Metabolic Confusion HIIT concept, a revolutionary way to break through plateaus and achieve sustained results.

Through his engaging writing style, Vincent C. Santos translates complex fitness principles into accessible guidance that readers can apply to their own lives. His book offers a comprehensive roadmap for individuals at all fitness levels, from beginners seeking to build a strong foundation to advanced enthusiasts pushing the boundaries of their capabilities.

But Vincent's impact goes beyond just fitness routines and meal plans. Recognizing the interconnectedness of physical and mental wellness, he dedicates a significant portion of his book to topics like stress management, mindfulness, and cultivating a positive mindset. Vincent believes that true success is achieved when we address the holistic needs of our bodies and minds.

As you embark on your journey through the pages of "Metabolic Confusion HIIT," you'll discover Vincent C. Santos's unwavering commitment to helping you achieve not only your fitness goals but also a vibrant and fulfilling life. His insights, strategies, and compassion will guide you through the challenges and triumphs of your transformation, reminding you that your potential knows no bounds when you align your efforts with purpose and intention.

Vincent C. Santos's approach is a testament to the fact that fitness isn't just a destination; it's a lifelong journey of growth, self-discovery, and becoming the best version of yourself.

TABLE OF CONTENT

Industry Experts Weigh In: Tips, Techniques, and Professional Advice

INTRODUCTION

For starters, I appreciate your interest in this book and your decision to read it. I really hope the information was insightful and helpful to you.

Understanding the Power of Metabolic Confusion HIIT

In the realm of fitness and wellness, there's a phenomenon that's been generating a buzz among enthusiasts and experts alike – Metabolic Confusion HIIT. This innovative approach combines the proven efficacy of High-Intensity Interval Training (HIIT) with a unique twist that keeps your body on its toes and your metabolism firing on all cylinders.

At its essence, metabolic confusion HIIT challenges the body's natural tendency to adapt and plateau. It thrives on the principle of variability, constantly changing the parameters of your workouts to prevent your metabolism from settling into a predictable rhythm. By embracing the concept of metabolic confusion, you can break free from the confines of conventional fitness routines and unlock a realm of accelerated fat loss, enhanced endurance, and the sculpting of lean muscle.

Imagine a workout regimen that refuses to let your body grow complacent. Each session becomes a strategic dance between intensity, rest, and recovery – a dance that triggers a cascade of physiological responses that work in harmony to amplify your results. The beauty of metabolic confusion HIIT lies in its ability to challenge both the mind and body, transforming your fitness journey into an exhilarating adventure where every session brings a new challenge and a fresh step toward your goals.

As you journey through the pages of this book, you'll discover the science that underpins metabolic confusion HIIT, the practical strategies to incorporate it into your routine, and the remarkable stories of individuals who have reaped the rewards of this cutting-edge approach. Get ready to step into a world of metabolic possibilities, where your potential knows no bounds and your body becomes a masterpiece in motion.

In the realm of fitness and wellness, a new frontier is emerging—one that promises to revolutionize the way we approach exercise and achieve our health goals. This chapter is your gateway to this exciting world of transformation—welcome to the realm of Metabolic Confusion HIIT.

Unveiling the Core Concepts

Metabolic Confusion HIIT is not just another fitness fad; it's a strategic and science-backed methodology designed to harness your body's innate potential for growth and change. At its heart are two intertwined concepts: High-Intensity Interval Training (HIIT) and metabolic confusion.

HIIT: Fueling the Fire

HIIT is the foundation upon which this revolution is built. We all know that pushing our limits through bursts of intense exercise followed by short recovery periods can yield incredible results. But with Metabolic Confusion HIIT, we take it several steps further. We dig deep into the science of intensity, discovering how to tailor it to our unique capacities to maximize gains and minimize risks.

Metabolic Confusion: The Game Changer

Now, imagine a realm where predictability is the enemy of progress. Metabolic Confusion throws your body into a delightful state of chaos—controlled chaos, that is. By strategically altering workout variables, such as exercise selection, intensity, and recovery times, we keep your metabolism on its toes. Your body never quite knows what's coming next, and that's where the magic happens. Plateaus? Bid them farewell. Stagnation? A thing of the past.

Significance and Intrigue

Why does this matter? Because your journey is unique. Your body is dynamic, and your goals are your own. Metabolic Confusion HIIT doesn't just offer a one-size-fits-all solution—it's a personalized roadmap to success. By the time you turn the last page of this book, you'll understand why this approach isn't just about sweat and muscle—it's a catalyst for holistic transformation.

Delve Deeper: What Awaits

The chapters that follow are your expedition guides through the landscape of Metabolic Confusion HIIT. We'll decode the science behind the method, laying bare the mechanisms that make it work. You'll become intimately familiar with crafting workouts that are as diverse as they are effective, and we'll explore the delicate interplay between exercise and nutrition.

Prepare to meet real individuals whose lives have been transformed by Metabolic Confusion HIIT. From beginners embarking on their fitness journey to seasoned athletes pushing the boundaries of their capabilities, their stories are proof that this approach holds immense promise.

So, fasten your seatbelt. The journey ahead is one of discovery, challenge, and fulfillment. You're about to uncover the true potential of your body and mind through the power of Metabolic Confusion HIIT. Let's embark on this adventure together.

The Science Behind Metabolic Confusion: How it Boosts Fat Loss and Fitness Gains

Metabolism and its Complexity:

Metabolism is the intricate web of biochemical processes that occur within your body to sustain life. It involves converting the food you eat into energy, building and repairing tissues, and managing waste. It's not just about the number of calories you consume and burn; it's influenced by various factors such as hormones, genetics, age, and body composition.

Variability and Adaptation:

Your body is a master at adaptation. When you engage in a consistent exercise routine, it becomes more efficient at performing those specific tasks. However, this efficiency can lead to plateaus in your progress. Metabolic Confusion HIIT disrupts this adaptation by introducing variability. By constantly changing workout variables like exercise type, intensity, duration, and rest intervals, you prevent your body from settling into a predictable pattern.

This variability keeps your metabolism engaged and continuously challenged.

Elevated Caloric Expenditure: The Afterburn Effect:
One of the standout features of Metabolic Confusion HIIT is its ability to elevate your caloric expenditure not just during the workout, but also after you've finished. This is known as the afterburn effect or excess post-exercise oxygen consumption (EPOC). During intense exercise, your body uses a significant amount of oxygen to restore itself to its pre-exercise state. This process requires energy, which means you continue to burn calories even after you're done working out. Metabolic Confusion HIIT's variable intensity and demand for increased oxygen contribute to a more prolonged afterburn, aiding in fat loss.

Challenging Muscle Fibers and Energy Systems:
Metabolic Confusion HIIT isn't just about cardio; it also targets different energy systems and muscle fibers. For instance, changing between high-intensity and moderate-intensity intervals engages both your

aerobic and anaerobic energy systems. This comprehensive workout approach stimulates various muscle fibers, enhancing your overall muscle development and functional fitness.

Increased Hormonal Response:

Intense exercise, especially with changing intensities, triggers a cascade of hormonal responses. Hormones like adrenaline and growth hormone play crucial roles in fat metabolism and muscle growth. Metabolic Confusion HIIT's challenging nature amplifies this hormonal response, leading to more efficient fat utilization and muscle repair.

Preventing Adaptation and Overtraining:

Traditional workouts might lead to overtraining or burnout as your body becomes accustomed to the same routines. Metabolic Confusion HIIT's ever-changing nature prevents this adaptation, reducing the risk of overtraining. This approach keeps your workouts fresh and exciting, preventing the monotony that can often lead to decreased motivation.

Summary and Preview:

Understanding the scientific principles behind Metabolic Confusion HIIT illuminates its potency. By introducing variability, challenging multiple energy systems, and triggering hormonal responses, this methodology transforms your body's response to exercise. As you progress through the subsequent chapters, you'll learn how to craft workouts that harness these principles, enabling you to embark on a journey of unprecedented fat loss, increased fitness gains, and a more robust, adaptable physique.

CHAPTER ONE

METABOLIC CONFUSION DEMYSTIFIED

Defining Metabolic Confusion: Unveiling the Core Concepts

In this chapter, we delve into the very essence of Metabolic Confusion, dissecting its core concepts to provide you with a clear understanding of what sets this methodology apart from traditional approaches to fitness. Get ready to embark on a journey that will reshape your perception of exercise and propel you toward unprecedented results.

The Foundation of Metabolic Confusion

At its heart, Metabolic Confusion is a revolutionary approach that challenges the body to reach new heights of performance and transformation. Unlike static routines that your body easily adapts to, Metabolic Confusion embraces the dynamic nature of your body's responses. It recognizes that your body's adaptability can be both a friend and a foe, and it leverages this knowledge to drive continuous progress.

Variable Intensity and Workouts that Adapt:

Metabolic Confusion is built upon the principle of variability. This means that no two workouts are the same. The intensity, duration, and types of exercises are intentionally varied, preventing your body from acclimating to a particular routine. This variation ignites a perpetual state of adaptation, forcing your body to engage different energy systems and muscle fibers.

The Role of Surprise: Keeping the Body Guessing:

Surprise is the cornerstone of Metabolic Confusion. Just as your body tends to plateau with repetitive routines, it thrives when introduced to unexpected challenges. Each workout becomes a puzzle your body eagerly solves, leading to improved calorie burn, muscle development, and enhanced overall fitness.

Timing and Recovery: The Art of Balancing:

In Metabolic Confusion, timing is everything. Intervals of high-intensity exercises are meticulously interspersed with periods of active recovery. This balanced approach ensures that your body doesn't veer into overtraining territory. It optimizes muscle repair, growth, and the efficient utilization of energy stores.

Metabolic Flexibility: A Holistic Approach:

Metabolic Confusion transcends the confines of individual workouts—it's a lifestyle that cultivates metabolic flexibility. Your body learns to efficiently switch between energy sources, from glucose to stored fat. This metabolic adaptability not only enhances fat loss but also sustains your energy levels throughout the day.

Harnessing the Power of Adaptation:

While Metabolic Confusion exploits the body's adaptive nature, it does so strategically. It keeps your body's responses dynamic, preventing it from reaching a plateau. Through constant adaptation, you'll experience continuous progress and avoid the dreaded fitness stagnation.

Summary and What Lies Ahead:

As you absorb the core concepts of Metabolic Confusion, you're laying the groundwork for a transformative journey. The chapters that follow will guide you through the practical application of these principles, equipping you with the tools to craft effective workouts, optimize nutrition, and embrace a lifestyle that fuels your body's potential. Prepare to redefine your approach to fitness and unlock a realm of unparalleled results. Welcome to the heart of Metabolic Confusion—where the journey to your best self truly begins.

The Benefits of Metabolic Confusion HIIT: Why It Works

Welcome to a chapter dedicated to unraveling the myriad benefits that make Metabolic Confusion HIIT a game-changing approach to fitness. Prepare to be enlightened as we explore the reasons behind its effectiveness and why it has garnered widespread attention as a transformative methodology.

Holistic Transformation: Beyond the Surface:

Metabolic Confusion HIIT isn't just about shedding pounds—it's about holistic transformation. This methodology recognizes that true fitness encompasses more than mere aesthetics. It's about optimizing your body's performance, enhancing your endurance, and building functional strength that translates into daily life.

Continuous Progress: Bypassing Plateaus:

One of the most frustrating roadblocks in traditional fitness routines is the plateau—an obstacle that often halts progress. Metabolic Confusion HIIT sidesteps this hurdle by keeping your body guessing. By embracing variability, your body never becomes accustomed to the routine, leading to continuous progress without stagnation.

Maximized Caloric Burn: During and After Workouts:

The magic of Metabolic Confusion HIIT lies in its ability to trigger an elevated calorie burn not just during the workout, but long after you've finished exercising. This phenomenon, known as the afterburn effect or excess post-exercise oxygen consumption (EPOC), means your body continues to burn calories even when you're at rest.

Preservation of Lean Muscle: The Right Kind of Loss:

Conventional weight loss often involves both fat and muscle loss. Metabolic Confusion HIIT, on the other hand, places a premium on preserving lean muscle mass. Its variable intensity and strategic rest intervals ensure that your body taps into stored fat for energy while safeguarding your hard-earned muscle.

Efficiency in Time: Short Workouts, Big Impact:

Modern life is busy, and carving out hours for exercise can be a challenge. Metabolic Confusion HIIT is tailored for efficiency, offering short yet intense workouts that deliver substantial results. By maximizing intensity within a shorter timeframe, it aligns with the demands of a busy lifestyle.

Cardiovascular Health: Elevating Endurance:

Metabolic Confusion HIIT isn't just about resistance training—it's a cardiovascular workout as well. Its varying intensities challenge your heart and lungs, enhancing cardiovascular health and boosting endurance. It's a two-for-one deal that efficiently targets multiple fitness dimensions.

Tailored for All Levels: Inclusivity in Fitness:

Whether you're a fitness novice or a seasoned athlete, Metabolic Confusion HIIT is designed for inclusivity. Workouts can be customized to match your fitness level and progressively scaled as you improve. It's a methodology that grows with you, ensuring every participant finds challenge and growth.

Fueling Motivation: Variety and Progress:

Variability isn't just a science-based concept—it's also a powerful motivational tool. The constant challenge presented by Metabolic Confusion HIIT keeps your workouts fresh, engaging both your mind and body. Every session brings a new puzzle to solve, fueling your motivation and commitment.

Your Transformation Awaits:

As you uncover the multitude of benefits that Metabolic Confusion HIIT offers, you're taking the first step toward a fitness journey that transcends conventional norms. Armed with this knowledge, you're ready to embrace the practical aspects of this methodology. The upcoming chapters will guide you through crafting workouts, optimizing nutrition, and sustaining your transformation. Prepare to unlock the full potential of your body, mind, and results with Metabolic Confusion HIIT.

CHAPTER TWO

HIIT ESSENTIALS

High-Intensity Interval Training (HIIT) Unpacked

Step into the world of High-Intensity Interval Training (HIIT), a cornerstone of the Metabolic Confusion HIIT approach. In this chapter, we'll dissect the nuances of HIIT, revealing its scientific foundations, benefits, and how it seamlessly integrates into the transformative journey you're embarking on.

Understanding HIIT: A Snapshot:

High-Intensity Interval Training, commonly known as HIIT, is a workout methodology that alternates between short bursts of intense exercise and periods of active recovery. This contrast between high-intensity and lower-intensity intervals is what makes HIIT both challenging and effective.

The Science Behind the Burn: EPOC:

HIIT isn't just about feeling the burn during the workout—it's about igniting a metabolic fire that lasts long after you've finished exercising. Excess post-exercise oxygen consumption (EPOC) is the phenomenon responsible for this prolonged calorie burn, and HIIT is a potent trigger for it.

Efficiency: Maximized Results in Minimal Time:

Modern life demands efficiency, and that's precisely what HIIT delivers. Short yet intense workouts allow you to achieve substantial fitness gains without spending hours at the gym. With Metabolic Confusion HIIT, these time-efficient workouts become even more dynamic and effective.

Cardiovascular and Aerobic Endurance: Pushing Boundaries:

HIIT isn't just about building muscle—it's also a powerful cardiovascular workout. The high-intensity intervals push your heart and lungs to work harder, enhancing your aerobic capacity and endurance. It's a cardiovascular boost that complements the muscle-building aspects of Metabolic Confusion HIIT.

Metabolic Adaptation: Efficiency in Action:

HIIT doesn't just torch calories—it restructures how your body utilizes energy. These short bursts of intense exercise challenge your body's energy systems, making them more efficient over time. This metabolic adaptation contributes to fat loss and overall fitness gains.

Customization for All Levels: Inclusivity in Intensity:

One of HIIT's strengths lies in its adaptability. It can be tailored to suit various fitness levels, making it accessible to both beginners and advanced athletes. This inclusivity aligns perfectly with the holistic approach of Metabolic Confusion HIIT.

Complementary to Metabolic Confusion: A Perfect Match:

HIIT is more than just a component of Metabolic Confusion—it's the heartbeat of the methodology. Its variable intensity intervals align seamlessly with the overarching goal of preventing adaptation and sparking continuous progress.

Elevating Your Fitness Arsenal:

As you unravel the intricacies of HIIT, you're adding a powerful tool to your fitness arsenal. The knowledge gained in this chapter primes you for the practical implementation of HIIT within the framework of Metabolic Confusion HIIT. The subsequent chapters will guide you through crafting dynamic workouts, fine-tuning your nutrition, and embracing a lifestyle that harnesses the full potential of HIIT and Metabolic Confusion. Get ready to elevate your workouts, amplify your results, and step into a realm of fitness that's anything but ordinary.

The Role of Intensity: How to Find Your Sweet Spot

Introducing the heart of effective training: intensity. In this chapter, we'll dissect the significance of intensity within the context of Metabolic Confusion HIIT. Discover how to gauge and optimize your efforts, ensuring you find the elusive "sweet spot" that maximizes results while safeguarding your well-being.

The Intensity Paradox: The Key to Progress:

Intensity is the driving force behind effective workouts. It's the fine line between pushing your limits and overexertion. We'll dive into the paradox of intensity—the delicate balance that makes all the difference in your fitness journey.

Understanding Your Intensity Zones: The Spectrum of Effort:

Intensity isn't a one-size-fits-all metric. It's a spectrum that ranges from light to maximal effort. We'll explore the different intensity zones, from low to high, and help you understand where each zone fits within the context of Metabolic Confusion HIIT.

Personalizing Intensity: Factors and Variables:

Your ideal intensity isn't solely determined by fitness charts or formulas—it's deeply personal. Factors like fitness level, age, and health conditions influence what constitutes a challenging yet sustainable effort for you. We'll guide you through personalizing your intensity for optimal results.

Effort and Progression: The Art of Stepping Up:

Consistently pushing your boundaries is essential for growth, but it should be a gradual progression. This section highlights the importance of progressively increasing intensity to prevent plateaus and ensure you're constantly challenging your body.

Listening to Your Body: The Wisdom of Sensation:

Your body communicates its limits through sensations like heart rate, breathing, and muscle fatigue. Learning to interpret these signals empowers you to adjust intensity on the fly, ensuring a safe and effective workout.

The Psychological Edge: Mental Intensity and Focus:

Intensity isn't just physical—it's also mental. Discover how harnessing mental intensity and focus can elevate your workouts. We'll delve into techniques to sharpen your mental state and channel your determination effectively.

Feedback and Adaptation: The Dynamic Nature of Intensity:

As you progress on your fitness journey, your body evolves, and so does your perception of intensity. We'll discuss the importance of continually assessing and adapting your intensity levels to match your evolving capabilities.

Finding Your Sweet Spot: Balancing Challenge and Sustainability:

The "sweet spot" is where challenge and sustainability intersect—a place where you push your limits while ensuring that your efforts are sustainable over the long term. We'll guide you through identifying and cultivating this sweet spot to unlock your full potential.

Empowering Your Training:

By grasping the role of intensity and learning how to navigate its intricacies, you're arming yourself with a powerful tool. The knowledge gained here will be the compass that guides you through crafting dynamic workouts and embracing a lifestyle that optimizes your Metabolic Confusion HIIT journey. Prepare to revolutionize your approach to training, harnessing the magic of intensity for transformative results.

CHAPTER THREE

THE METABOLIC CONFUSION FACTOR

How Metabolic Confusion Takes HIIT to the Next Level

"Metabolic Confusion" in the context of HIIT could potentially refer to the idea of enhancing the effectiveness of your High-Intensity Interval Training (HIIT) workouts by introducing variability and unpredictability in certain aspects of your training routine. The aim would be to challenge your body in new ways, prevent adaptation, and potentially achieve better fitness results. Here's a more detailed breakdown of how this concept could work:

Varying Intensity Levels: Instead of sticking to a consistent level of high intensity throughout your entire HIIT workout, you could alternate between different intensity levels. For example, you might have some intervals where you go all-out with maximum effort, while others could be slightly less intense. This variation challenges different energy systems and muscle fibers, potentially leading to greater improvements in overall fitness.

Changing Exercise Selection: Instead of always using the same set of exercises in your HIIT routine, you can introduce new exercises that target different muscle groups. This approach prevents your body from getting too accustomed to specific movements and muscle patterns, which can lead to plateaus in progress.

Adjusting Work-to-Rest Ratios: Traditionally, HIIT involves short bursts of intense exercise followed by equally short rest periods. However, with metabolic confusion, you might vary the duration of work and rest intervals. This keeps your body guessing about when the next intense effort will come and can lead to different physiological adaptations.

Incorporating Different Modalities: Mixing different types of exercises within the same HIIT session can create a higher level of metabolic confusion. For example, combining cardio-focused exercises like sprinting with strength-focused exercises like bodyweight resistance movements can challenge your body's systems in novel ways.

Periodization and Progression: Metabolic confusion might involve incorporating periodization into your training plan. Periodization is the organized approach of cycling your training variables (like intensity, volume, and exercise selection) over defined periods. By gradually increasing the demands of your workouts over time and then resetting them, you can continue making progress while avoiding plateaus.

Neuromuscular Adaptations: Changing variables in your HIIT routine could also influence neuromuscular adaptations. These adaptations affect how efficiently your nervous system communicates with your muscles, potentially leading to improved coordination, balance, and overall performance.

It's important to emphasize that while the idea of "Metabolic Confusion" can sound promising, the effectiveness of this concept would likely depend on several factors, including individual fitness goals, training experience, and the specific adaptations your body makes.

Creating Variability: The Key to Preventing Plateaus

Creating variability in your workouts is indeed a key strategy to prevent plateaus and continuously make progress in your fitness journey. When your body adapts to a specific exercise routine or intensity level, it becomes more efficient at performing those tasks, which can lead to stagnation in your results. By introducing variability, you challenge your body in new ways and encourage ongoing improvements. Here are some strategies to create variability and prevent plateaus:

Exercise Selection: Rotate through a variety of exercises that target the same muscle groups. For example, if you've been doing regular squats, switch to sumo squats, goblet squats, or Bulgarian split squats. This variation engages muscles differently and prevents overuse.

Intensity Levels: Change the intensity of your workouts. For instance, you can alternate between high-intensity workouts and moderate-intensity sessions. This approach challenges different energy systems and prevents your body from adapting to a single intensity level.

Work-to-Rest Ratios: Adjust the work-to-rest ratios in your HIIT workouts. You can have shorter intervals with higher intensity followed by longer rest periods, and vice versa. This keeps your body guessing and encourages different physiological adaptations.

Incorporate New Modalities: Introduce new forms of exercise or activities you haven't tried before. If you're used to traditional cardio, try incorporating swimming, cycling, or a dance class. New modalities engage different muscle groups and movement patterns.

Progressive Overload: Continuously challenge your body by gradually increasing the demands of your workouts. This could involve increasing weights, reps, or intensity over time. Progressive overload ensures your body doesn't get complacent.

Periodization: Organize your training into phases with different focuses. For example, have strength-focused phases, endurance-focused phases, and power-focused phases. This helps prevent overtraining and allows for specific adaptations to occur.

Cross-Training: Engage in activities outside your primary workout routine. Cross-training can include yoga, Pilates, hiking, or any activity that complements your main workouts. It prevents overuse injuries and provides mental refreshment.

Unilateral Movements: Include unilateral exercises that work one side of your body at a time. This addresses muscle imbalances and challenges your core stability.

Change Equipment: If you primarily use machines, switch to free weights or resistance bands. Different equipment engages stabilizing muscles and can lead to new gains.

Mind-Muscle Connection: Focus on your mind-muscle connection during workouts. Concentrate on the muscles you're working and perform exercises with precision and control. This can lead to improved muscle activation and growth.

Nutrition and Recovery: Plateaus can also result from inadequate nutrition or recovery. Ensure you're fueling your body properly and getting sufficient rest to support your workouts.

Remember that while variability is important, it's essential to maintain proper form and avoid overloading yourself too quickly, which can lead to injuries. If possible, consult a fitness professional or personal trainer to design a well-rounded and progressive workout plan tailored to your goals and fitness level.

CHAPTER FOUR

THE METABOLIC CONFUSION HIIT METHOD

Crafting Effective Workouts: Structure and Principles

Here's an example of how to craft an effective Metabolic Confusion HIIT workout using the principles and structure.

Workout: Full-Body Power Fusion

Warm-up: 5 minutes of dynamic stretches and light cardio to prepare your body.

Interval Variation:

High-Intensity Burst: 30 seconds of Burpees (Maximum effort)

Moderate-Intensity Interval: 45 seconds of Jumping Jacks (Medium effort)

High-Intensity Burst: 30 seconds of Kettlebell Swings (Maximum effort)

Moderate-Intensity Interval: 45 seconds of Mountain Climbers (Medium effort)

Exercise Diversity:

Strength Interval: 40 seconds of Push-Ups (Maximum effort)

Cardio Interval: 60 seconds of Sprints (Maximum effort, either on a treadmill or outdoor)

Hybrid Intervals:

Hybrid Interval: 30 seconds of Squat Jumps followed by 30 seconds of Push Press (Using dumbbells or resistance bands)

Rest Intervals:

Active Recovery: 60 seconds of brisk walking or slow jogging

Progressive Overload:

Progressive Intensity: Repeat Interval 1 (Burpees) and Interval 2 (Jumping Jacks) with 5-10% increase in intensity (faster pace, higher jump, etc.)

Structured Chaos:

Spontaneous Challenge: Choose an exercise that you haven't included yet and perform it for 1 minute with maximum effort.

Cool-down: 5-10 minutes of static stretches and deep breathing to cool down and promote recovery.

Personalization and Mind-Body Connection:

Throughout the workout, focus on your breathing, maintain good form, and mentally engage in each interval. Visualize your goals and use positive self-talk to push through challenging moments.

Note: The intervals, exercises, and duration mentioned above are for illustrative purposes. You should tailor the workout to your fitness level, preferences, and any equipment you have available. Remember that safety and proper form are paramount—listen to your body and adjust intensity as needed.

By applying the principles of variability, exercise diversity, progressive overload, and personalization, this example workout embraces the essence of Metabolic Confusion HIIT. It challenges different muscle groups, energy systems, and intensities, ensuring continuous progress and preventing plateaus.

Timing Matters: Intervals, Rest, and Progression

Absolutely, timing plays a crucial role in optimizing the effectiveness of your workouts, especially when it comes to intervals, rest, and progression. Here's how you can strategically manage these aspects for better results:

1. Intervals:

High-Intensity Interval Training (HIIT) relies on alternating between periods of high-intensity exercise and periods of lower-intensity activity or rest. The timing of these intervals influences the stress placed on your body and the adaptations it undergoes.

Interval Length: The length of your high-intensity intervals will depend on the exercise and your fitness level. It could range from 20 seconds to 2 minutes or more. Shorter intervals focus on anaerobic power, while longer intervals target aerobic endurance.

Work-to-Rest Ratio: The ratio of work to rest is important. A common ratio is 1:1, where your work interval is as long as your rest interval. For example, if you sprint for 30 seconds, you rest for 30 seconds. You can manipulate this ratio based on your goals. Shorter rest periods make the workout more challenging, while longer rest periods aid recovery.

Progressive Overload: Just as with weights, you can apply progressive overload to intervals. Increase the intensity or duration of your intervals gradually to keep pushing your limits and preventing adaptation.

2. Rest:

Rest intervals are crucial in allowing your body to recover enough to perform optimally during the next high-intensity interval. The timing and quality of your rest periods impact the overall effectiveness of your workout.

Active Rest: Instead of complete rest during your rest intervals, consider performing low-intensity movements. This helps keep your heart rate elevated and contributes to the overall calorie burn of the workout.

Recovery: Make sure to allow enough recovery time between high-intensity sessions. Overtraining can lead to burnout and injuries. Listen to your body and prioritize recovery days.

3. Progression:

To continually improve and prevent plateaus, you need a well-structured progression plan that gradually increases the demands on your body.

Increasing Intensity: As you become more conditioned, gradually increase the intensity of your high-intensity intervals. This could involve increasing speed, resistance, or effort.

Changing Variables: Periodically change the variables in your workout, such as exercise selection, intensity levels, and work-to-rest ratios. This prevents your body from adapting too quickly.

Frequency and Volume: Progression isn't just about intensity. You can increase the frequency (number of sessions per week) or volume (total work done in a session) as well.

Deload Weeks: Incorporate deload weeks where you reduce the intensity or volume. This allows your body to recover and come back stronger.

Remember, individual responses to timing and progression vary, so it's essential to listen to your body, avoid overtraining, and adapt your approach based on how you feel and the results you're achieving. If you're new to interval training or have specific fitness goals, consulting a fitness professional can help you design a customized plan that takes into account your fitness level and objectives.

CHAPTER FIVE

WORKOUT ROUTINES

Beginner's Metabolic Confusion HIIT: Building the Foundation

Creating a beginner's Metabolic Confusion HIIT (High-Intensity Interval Training) routine involves incorporating variability into your workouts while focusing on building a solid foundation. Here's a step-by-step guide to help you get started:

1. Consult a Professional:

Before beginning any new exercise program, especially if you're new to HIIT, it's advisable to consult a fitness professional or healthcare provider to ensure that your workout plan aligns with your fitness level and any potential health considerations.

2. Warm-Up:

Start with a dynamic warm-up to prepare your muscles and joints for the upcoming intensity. Include movements like arm circles, leg swings, hip rotations, and light cardio to increase your heart rate gradually.

3. Exercise Selection:

Choose a mix of basic exercises that engage large muscle groups and are suitable for beginners. Focus on movements that you can perform with proper form to prevent injuries.

Sample exercises:

Bodyweight squats

Push-ups (modified if needed)

Lunges

Jumping jacks

High knees

Mountain climbers

4. Intervals:

Design your HIIT routine using different interval lengths and work-to-rest ratios. For beginners, start with longer work intervals and longer rest intervals to allow sufficient recovery.

Sample routine:

30 seconds of exercise

60 seconds of rest (active recovery like walking or slow jogging)

As you progress, you can decrease the rest intervals and increase the intensity of your exercises.

5. Exercise Variation:

Incorporate exercise variation to challenge different muscle groups and movement patterns. For instance, if you start with bodyweight squats, the next interval could involve lunges.

6. Progressive Overload:

Over time, gradually increase the intensity or duration of your work intervals. As you become more comfortable, you can experiment with shorter rest intervals.

7. Full-Body Emphasis:

Since you're building a foundation, focus on full-body exercises that engage multiple muscle groups. This approach provides a balanced workout and improves overall strength and endurance.

8. Proper Form:

Maintain proper form throughout your exercises. Quality movement is more important than speed. This helps prevent injuries and ensures you're effectively targeting the intended muscles.

9. Recovery:

Adequate recovery is essential, especially for beginners. Allow at least 48 hours between intense HIIT sessions to let your body recover and adapt.

10. Incorporate Mobility and Flexibility:

Include mobility exercises and gentle stretching in your routine to improve flexibility and joint health. This can enhance your overall fitness experience.

11. Listen to Your Body:

Pay attention to how your body responds. If you experience pain or discomfort, adjust your workout accordingly. It's okay to start slowly and gradually increase the intensity.

12. Cool Down:

After completing your HIIT session, cool down with static stretches and deep breathing to help your body transition back to a resting state.

Remember, the key to success with Metabolic Confusion HIIT, especially as a beginner, is to start at your own pace, focus on proper form, and progress gradually. As you become more comfortable and experienced, you can adjust variables like interval lengths, intensity, and rest intervals to keep challenging your body and preventing plateaus.

Intermediate Workouts: Pushing Boundaries and Elevating Results

Transitioning from a beginner to an intermediate level in your workouts involves pushing your boundaries while maintaining a strong focus on form and safety. Here's a guide on creating intermediate-level workouts to elevate your results:

1. Assess Readiness:

Before progressing to intermediate workouts, ensure you have a solid foundation of strength, cardiovascular fitness, and proper exercise technique. If you're unsure, consider seeking guidance from a fitness professional.

2. Intensity and Complexity:

Intermediate workouts involve increasing the intensity and complexity of your exercises. This can include using heavier weights, incorporating more compound movements, and trying more advanced variations.

3. Split Routine:

Consider moving from full-body workouts to a split routine. Focus on specific muscle groups on different days, allowing for greater volume and intensity per muscle group.

4. Incorporate Compound Movements:

Include compound movements that work multiple muscle groups simultaneously. These exercises, such as squats, deadlifts, bench presses, and pull-ups, are effective for building strength and burning calories.

5. Progressive Overload:

Continue to apply progressive overload by gradually increasing the resistance, repetitions, or intensity of your exercises. This keeps your muscles adapting and growing.

6. High-Intensity Interval Training (HIIT):

Continue with HIIT, but consider shortening your rest intervals or increasing the intensity of your work intervals. This challenges your cardiovascular fitness and boosts calorie burn.

7. Complex Training:

Incorporate complex training, which combines heavy strength training with explosive exercises. For instance, pair a heavy squat with box jumps.

8. Periodization:

Implement a periodization plan that includes phases of different focuses. This could involve strength-building phases, hypertrophy phases (muscle growth), and power-focused phases.

9. Mobility and Flexibility:

As the intensity increases, don't neglect mobility and flexibility work. Maintaining good joint mobility and flexibility is essential for preventing injuries and improving performance.

10. Recovery and Nutrition:

Prioritize recovery through proper nutrition, hydration, and adequate sleep. Recovery becomes more critical as you challenge yourself with higher intensity workouts.

11. Monitor Progress:

Keep track of your workouts, weights lifted, and improvements in terms of endurance and strength. This helps you see your progress and make informed adjustments.

12. Challenge Mental Limits:

Intermediate workouts not only test your physical limits but also your mental resilience. Push yourself outside of your comfort zone, but listen to your body and avoid overtraining.

13. Rest and Active Recovery:

Include proper rest days and active recovery sessions. Your body needs time to repair and grow stronger.

14. Cross-Training:

Incorporate cross-training activities like swimming, cycling, or yoga to provide variety and challenge different muscle groups.

15. Form and Technique:

Maintain impeccable form and technique throughout your exercises. Poor form can lead to injuries and hinder your progress.

As an intermediate level exerciser, you have a solid foundation and can safely introduce more complex exercises and training methodologies. However, it's essential to continue learning and adapting your approach. If possible, consult with a fitness professional to design a personalized program that aligns with your goals and current fitness level.

Advanced Challenges: Maximizing Fat Burn and Performance Gains

Advancing to an advanced fitness level involves maximizing fat burn and performance gains through strategic training, nutrition, and recovery strategies. Here's how to approach these challenges:

1. Advanced Training Techniques:

Incorporate advanced training techniques to further challenge your body and stimulate fat loss and muscle growth.

Drop Sets: Perform multiple sets of an exercise with decreasing weights, pushing your muscles to fatigue.

Supersets and Circuits: Combine different exercises with minimal rest between sets to increase intensity and calorie burn.

Negatives and Eccentrics: Focus on the lowering phase of an exercise, which can increase muscle tension and metabolic demand.

Plyometrics: Integrate explosive movements like box jumps and plyometric push-ups to elevate your heart rate and improve power.

2. High-Intensity Cardio Variations:

Experiment with more advanced high-intensity cardio workouts to boost fat burn and cardiovascular fitness.

Tabata Intervals: Perform 20 seconds of all-out exercise followed by 10 seconds of rest, repeated for 4 minutes.

Interval Pyramids: Alternate between short, intense bursts and longer rest periods in a pyramid-like structure.

3. Strength Periodization:

Follow a structured strength periodization plan that cycles through different phases to target different aspects of performance and muscle growth.

Hypertrophy Phase: Focus on moderate weights and higher reps to stimulate muscle growth.

Strength Phase: Increase weight and reduce reps to build maximal strength.

Power Phase: Incorporate explosive movements to enhance power output.

4. Advanced Nutrition Strategies:

Fine-tune your nutrition to support fat loss and performance gains.

Macronutrient Timing: Time your intake of carbs and proteins around workouts for optimal performance and recovery.

Carb Cycling: Alternate between high and low carbohydrate days to manage energy levels and fat loss.

Protein Intake: Consume sufficient protein to support muscle repair and growth.

5. Recovery and Regeneration:

Prioritize recovery to avoid overtraining and enhance performance.

Active Recovery: Incorporate active recovery sessions like yoga, stretching, or light swimming.

Foam Rolling: Use foam rolling and self-massage to release muscle tension and improve mobility.

Sleep Quality: Aim for 7-9 hours of quality sleep each night to support recovery and hormone balance.

6. Advanced Tracking and Measurement:

Keep detailed records of your workouts, nutrition, and progress.

Tracking Workouts: Note weights, reps, and sets to ensure progressive overload.

Body Measurements: Track changes in body composition through measurements, photos, or body scans.

7. Mind-Muscle Connection:

Cultivate a strong mind-muscle connection during workouts to optimize muscle activation.

Focus and Visualization: Concentrate on the muscle being worked and visualize its contraction during exercises.

8. Mental Resilience:

At an advanced level, mental strength is crucial. Pushing through plateaus and overcoming challenges requires mental resilience.

9. Avoid Overtraining:

While pushing boundaries is essential, avoid overtraining by listening to your body, incorporating deload weeks, and getting adequate rest.

10. Seek Professional Guidance:

Consider working with a fitness coach or personal trainer who specializes in advanced training to create a customized plan that aligns with your goals and challenges.

Remember that advanced training requires a solid foundation, so progress incrementally and prioritize safety and proper form. As always, individual responses to training and nutrition vary, so what works for one person may not work for another. Continuously educate yourself and adapt your strategies based on your body's responses and your goals.

CHAPTER SIX

FUELING YOUR SUCCESS

Nutrition for Metabolic Confusion HIIT: What to Eat and When

Nutrition plays a vital role in supporting your Metabolic Confusion HIIT workouts and maximizing their effectiveness. The right foods at the right times can fuel your workouts, aid recovery, and contribute to fat loss and muscle gain. Here's a breakdown of what to eat and when for optimal results:

Before Your Workout:

Carbohydrates: Consume complex carbohydrates 1-2 hours before your workout. Carbs provide energy for your high-intensity intervals.

Protein: Include a moderate amount of protein to support muscle maintenance and repair during your workout.

Hydration: Begin hydrating well before your workout. Dehydration can impact performance.

Examples:

Whole-grain toast with peanut butter

Oatmeal with berries and a scoop of protein powder

Greek yogurt with fruit

During Your Workout:

Hydration: Sip water throughout your workout to stay hydrated, especially during intense intervals.

After Your Workout:

Protein: Consume protein within an hour after your workout to support muscle recovery and growth.

Carbohydrates: Include carbs to replenish glycogen stores and aid recovery.

Examples:

Grilled chicken with quinoa and vegetables

Rice cakes with lean turkey and avocado

Protein shake with banana and almond milk

Throughout the Day:

Balanced Meals: Focus on balanced meals that include lean protein, complex carbohydrates, healthy fats, and plenty of vegetables.

Healthy Fats: Incorporate sources of healthy fats like avocados, nuts, seeds, and olive oil. These fats support overall health and provide sustained energy.

Fruits and Vegetables: Aim to include a variety of colorful fruits and vegetables to provide essential vitamins, minerals, and antioxidants.

Frequent Meals: Eat smaller, frequent meals throughout the day to maintain steady energy levels.

Hydration:

Water Intake: Drink water consistently throughout the day to stay hydrated. Proper hydration supports digestion, metabolism, and performance.

Post-Workout Nutrition Timing:

The post-workout window is crucial for recovery and muscle growth. Consuming a meal or snack containing both protein and carbohydrates within an hour after your workout is ideal.

Supplements:

While whole foods should be the foundation of your nutrition, supplements can support your efforts:

Protein Powder: Whey or plant-based protein powders can be convenient for post-workout recovery.

BCAAs (Branched-Chain Amino Acids): These can be consumed during or after your workout to support muscle recovery and reduce muscle breakdown.

Individualization:

Remember that nutrition is highly individual. What works best for you may differ from others. Pay attention to how your body responds to different foods and timings.

Sample Day:

Breakfast: Oatmeal with berries and a scoop of protein powder.

Snack: Greek yogurt with a handful of almonds.

Lunch: Grilled chicken with quinoa and vegetables.

Snack: Apple slices with nut butter.

Dinner: Baked salmon with sweet potatoes and steamed broccoli.

It's recommended to consult a registered dietitian or nutritionist who can provide personalized guidance based on your goals, preferences, and any dietary restrictions. Additionally, keep in mind that consistency in both your workouts and nutrition is key to achieving long-term results.

The Role of Macros: Protein, Carbs, and Fats in Your Regimen

Understanding the role of macronutrients (protein, carbohydrates, and fats) in your regimen is crucial for optimizing your fitness goals, whether it's fat loss, muscle gain, or overall performance. Each macronutrient serves specific functions in your body and should be balanced according to your individual needs and goals.

1. Protein:

Function: Protein is essential for muscle repair, growth, and maintenance. It also supports immune function, enzyme production, and the creation of hormones.

Role in HIIT: Adequate protein intake is crucial for muscle recovery after intense workouts. It helps repair damaged muscle fibers and supports muscle protein synthesis.

Recommended Intake: Aim for about 1.2 to 2.0 grams of protein per kilogram of body weight per day, especially if you're engaged in intense workouts.

Sources: Lean meats, poultry, fish, eggs, dairy, legumes, tofu, and protein supplements.

2. Carbohydrates:

Function: Carbohydrates are your body's primary source of energy. They fuel your workouts and help replenish glycogen stores in muscles.

Role in HIIT: Carbohydrates provide the energy needed for high-intensity intervals and help sustain your performance throughout the workout.

Recommended Intake: The amount of carbs you need depends on your activity level and goals. Aim for complex carbs like whole grains, fruits, and vegetables.

Timing: Focus on consuming carbs before and after your workouts for energy and recovery.

3. Fats:

Function: Fats are essential for overall health, including hormone production, brain function, and cell structure. They also provide a concentrated source of energy.

Role in HIIT: Healthy fats support long-lasting energy during workouts and help maintain overall health.

Recommended Intake: Aim for a balance of healthy fats, including monounsaturated fats (olive oil, avocados), polyunsaturated fats (nuts, seeds, fatty fish), and a moderate amount of saturated fats.

Timing: Include fats in your meals, but be mindful of portion sizes as they are calorie-dense.

Balancing Macros for Your Goals:

Fat Loss: Focus on a moderate calorie deficit by reducing overall calorie intake. Maintain a higher protein intake to preserve muscle mass and support fat loss. Carbohydrates should be adjusted to support your workouts while promoting fat loss.

Muscle Gain: Prioritize protein intake to support muscle growth and recovery. Carbohydrates are important to fuel workouts and aid in recovery. Include healthy fats for overall health and energy.

Performance: Balance your macronutrients to support your energy needs during intense workouts. Carbohydrates are especially important to fuel high-intensity efforts, while protein helps with recovery and muscle maintenance.

Individualization:

The optimal balance of macronutrients varies from person to person based on factors such as activity level, metabolism, body composition, and goals. Tracking your intake and observing how your body responds can help you fine-tune your macro ratios.

Consult a Professional:

If you're unsure about how to balance your macros, consider consulting a registered dietitian or nutritionist. They can provide personalized guidance based on your unique needs and help you create a nutrition plan that aligns with your fitness goals.

CHAPTER SEVEN

RECOVERY AND REJUVENATION

The Importance of Recovery: Strategies for Optimal Healing

Recovery is a critical aspect of any fitness regimen. Proper recovery strategies are essential for allowing your body to heal, adapt, and perform at its best. Here are key strategies to ensure optimal healing and recovery:

1. Rest and Sleep:

Quality Sleep: Aim for 7-9 hours of quality sleep each night. Sleep is when your body repairs tissues, balances hormones, and supports overall recovery.

2. Nutrition:

Post-Workout Nutrition: Consume a balanced meal or snack containing protein and carbohydrates within an hour after your workout to support muscle recovery and replenish glycogen stores.

Hydration: Stay hydrated throughout the day to support circulation, nutrient delivery, and overall bodily functions.

3. Active Recovery:

Low-Intensity Activities: Engage in gentle activities like walking, swimming, or cycling at a low intensity on rest days. This promotes blood flow and helps alleviate muscle soreness.

4. Foam Rolling and Self-Myofascial Release:

Foam Rolling: Use a foam roller to release muscle tension and improve flexibility. This can enhance recovery and reduce muscle soreness.

5. Stretching and Mobility Work:

Static Stretching: Incorporate static stretches after your workout to improve flexibility and prevent muscle tightness.

Dynamic Stretching: Use dynamic stretches before your workout to warm up your muscles and increase blood flow.

6. Contrast Baths or Cold/Hot Therapy:

Contrast Baths: Alternate between cold and hot water immersion to reduce muscle soreness and improve circulation.

Cold Packs and Hot Packs: Apply cold packs to reduce inflammation and hot packs to relax tight muscles.

7. Active Lifestyle:

Consistent Movement: Incorporate daily movement, even on rest days. This helps maintain joint mobility and prevent stiffness.

8. Mindfulness and Stress Management:

Mindfulness Practices: Engage in practices like meditation, deep breathing, or yoga to reduce stress. Elevated stress levels can hinder recovery.

9. Periodization and Deload Weeks:

Periodization: Incorporate periods of increased intensity followed by deload weeks with reduced volume or intensity. This prevents overtraining and supports recovery.

10. Listen to Your Body:

Body Signals: Pay attention to your body's signals. If you're experiencing persistent fatigue, soreness, or signs of overtraining, it's important to adjust your training intensity.

11. Professional Support:

Physical Therapy: If you have specific muscle imbalances or injuries, consider consulting a physical therapist for guidance on recovery exercises and strategies.

Massage Therapy: Professional massage can help release muscle tension and improve circulation.

12. Hygiene and Infection Prevention:

Cleanliness: Ensure you maintain good hygiene and cleanliness to prevent infections, especially if you're using shared gym equipment.

Remember, recovery is not a one-size-fits-all approach. Factors such as your fitness level, age, and the intensity of your workouts influence the recovery strategies that work best for you. Prioritize recovery as an integral part of your fitness journey to prevent burnout, enhance performance, and promote overall well-being.

Sleep, Stress, and Mindfulness: Balancing Your Wellbeing

Balancing sleep, managing stress, and practicing mindfulness are crucial for overall well-being and maintaining a healthy lifestyle. Let's delve deeper into each aspect and explore strategies to find harmony among them:

1. Sleep:

Prioritize Consistent Sleep Schedule: Aim to go to bed and wake up at the same times every day, even on weekends. This helps regulate your body's internal clock and improve sleep quality.

Create a Sleep-Conducive Environment: Make your sleep space comfortable, dark, and quiet. Consider using blackout curtains and minimizing noise disruptions.

Establish a Relaxing Bedtime Routine: Engage in calming activities before bed, such as reading, taking a warm bath, or practicing deep breathing exercises.

Limit Screen Time: Reduce exposure to screens (phones, tablets, computers) at least an hour before bedtime. The blue light emitted by screens can interfere with your body's production of the sleep-inducing hormone melatonin.

2. Stress Management:

Identify Stressors: Recognize the sources of stress in your life and work on addressing or minimizing them.

Practice Time Management: Organize your tasks and priorities to avoid feeling overwhelmed. Break down larger tasks into smaller, manageable steps.

Regular Physical Activity: Engage in regular exercise to release endorphins, which are natural stress-relievers.

Deep Breathing and Relaxation Techniques: Practice deep breathing exercises, progressive muscle relaxation, or guided imagery to calm your nervous system and reduce stress.

Healthy Boundaries: Learn to say no when necessary and set healthy boundaries to prevent overcommitting yourself.

3. Mindfulness:

Mindful Meditation: Dedicate time each day to mindfulness meditation. Focus your attention on your breath, bodily sensations, or a specific mantra.

Mindful Eating: Pay attention to the taste, texture, and smell of your food. Eat slowly and savor each bite.

Mindful Awareness: Practice being fully present in your daily activities. Engage your senses and observe your surroundings without judgment.

Nature Connection: Spend time in nature and engage with the natural world. This can have a grounding and calming effect on your mind.

Gratitude Practice: Regularly take a moment to reflect on things you're grateful for. This practice can shift your focus to positive aspects of your life.

Balancing All Three:

Morning Routine: Begin your day with a mindful activity, such as stretching, deep breathing, or a short meditation.

Scheduled Breaks: Incorporate short breaks throughout your day to practice mindfulness, stretch, or engage in breathing exercises.

Technology Use: Set boundaries on technology use, especially in the evening, to promote relaxation and better sleep.

Prioritize Self-Care: Ensure you allocate time for self-care activities that bring you joy and relaxation.

Seek Support: If managing sleep, stress, and mindfulness feels overwhelming, consider seeking guidance from a healthcare professional or a therapist.

Remember that finding balance is an ongoing journey, and it's normal to have fluctuations in these aspects based on life circumstances. The key is to cultivate awareness, make intentional choices, and prioritize your well-being. Gradually integrating these strategies into your daily routine can lead to a more balanced and fulfilling lifestyle.

CHAPTER EIGHT

REAL-LIFE TRANSFORMATIONS

Success Stories: How Metabolic Confusion HIIT Changed Lives

Success Story 1: Sarah's Transformation Through Metabolic Confusion HIIT

Meet Sarah, a busy professional who struggled with weight gain and low energy due to her sedentary job. Frustrated by fad diets and unsustainable workout routines, she discovered the power of Metabolic Confusion HIIT.

Sarah's Metabolic Confusion Journey:

After researching effective fitness strategies, Sarah decided to try Metabolic Confusion HIIT. With the guidance of a fitness coach, she carefully crafted a workout plan that combined high-intensity intervals with variability in exercises and intensity levels.

Results:

Weight Loss: Within a few months of consistent Metabolic Confusion HIIT workouts, Sarah shed the extra pounds that had been weighing her down for years.

Increased Energy: Sarah noticed a significant improvement in her energy levels throughout the day. She was no longer feeling sluggish during her work hours.

Muscle Definition: The combination of strength-focused intervals and active recovery helped Sarah build lean muscle mass, giving her a more toned and defined physique.

Confidence Boost: As her body transformed, Sarah's confidence soared. She felt proud of her accomplishments and gained a positive outlook on life.

Life Transformation:

Sarah's success with Metabolic Confusion HIIT extended beyond physical changes. She became more disciplined in her fitness routine, learned to listen to her body, and developed a sustainable lifestyle that allowed her to maintain her results.

Today, Sarah is an inspiration to her friends and colleagues. She continues to enjoy the benefits of Metabolic Confusion HIIT, keeping her body strong, her energy levels high, and her spirit lifted.

Success Story 2: Mark's Journey to Optimal Performance with Metabolic Confusion HIIT

Mark, a competitive athlete and fitness enthusiast, hit a plateau in his training routine. Seeking a new challenge, he turned to Metabolic Confusion HIIT and witnessed incredible changes.

Mark's Metabolic Confusion Journey:

As an experienced athlete, Mark understood the importance of pushing boundaries. He revamped his routine with Metabolic Confusion HIIT, incorporating varied intervals, exercises, and intensity levels to keep his body guessing.

Results:

Performance Breakthrough: Metabolic Confusion HIIT introduced a new level of intensity to Mark's training. He achieved personal bests in his speed, strength, and endurance metrics.

Lean Muscle Gain: Mark's body composition improved as he built lean muscle mass and reduced body fat. His muscles became more defined, contributing to his athletic aesthetics.

Enhanced Recovery: The strategic incorporation of active recovery intervals allowed Mark to maintain optimal performance without overtraining or risking injury.

Mental Toughness: Metabolic Confusion HIIT challenged not only Mark's physical abilities but also his mental resilience. He developed mental toughness and focus that translated to all aspects of his life.

Life Transformation:

Mark's dedication to Metabolic Confusion HIIT reinvigorated his passion for fitness. He found a renewed sense of purpose and discovered the true potential of his body. As a coach, he now shares his knowledge and success with others, inspiring them to push their boundaries and achieve greatness.

These success stories illustrate how Metabolic Confusion HIIT can have transformative effects on individuals of varying backgrounds and fitness levels. By embracing variability, pushing limits, and embracing a holistic approach to well-being, these individuals experienced positive changes that extended beyond physical appearance to impact their overall quality of life.

Success Story 3: Maria's Metabolic Confusion HIIT Journey to Balanced Living

Maria, a mother of two and a busy professional, struggled to find time for herself amidst her hectic schedule. Feeling drained and unhappy with her fitness level, she turned to Metabolic Confusion HIIT to reclaim her health and happiness.

Maria's Metabolic Confusion Journey:

Determined to make a change, Maria embarked on her Metabolic Confusion HIIT journey. She created a flexible workout plan that incorporated short but intense intervals, ensuring she could fit her workouts into her busy days.

Results:

Time Efficiency: Metabolic Confusion HIIT's shorter, intense workouts proved perfect for Maria's schedule. She no longer had to spend hours at the gym to achieve results.

Increased Stamina: Over time, Maria's stamina and endurance skyrocketed. Everyday tasks became easier, and she found herself more energized to take on her responsibilities.

Stress Relief: The structured workout routine allowed Maria to channel her stress into her workouts. She noticed improved mental clarity and an overall more positive outlook.

Balanced Lifestyle: Metabolic Confusion HIIT encouraged Maria to make healthier food choices and prioritize self-care. She found a balance between her family, work, and personal well-being.

Life Transformation:

Maria's transformation extended beyond her physical fitness. As she embraced Metabolic Confusion HIIT, she discovered a newfound appreciation for her body's capabilities. She became a role model for her children, demonstrating the importance of staying active and taking care of oneself.

Now, Maria thrives as a vibrant, energetic woman who values her well-being and radiates positivity. Her journey illustrates that even amidst life's demands, incorporating Metabolic Confusion HIIT can lead to remarkable transformations in both body and mind.

Success Story 4: Jason's Metabolic Confusion HIIT Journey to Overcoming Plateaus

Jason, a dedicated fitness enthusiast and avid weightlifter, found himself stuck in a training plateau. Frustrated by his lack of progress, he turned to Metabolic Confusion HIIT as a way to break through barriers and achieve new heights.

Jason's Metabolic Confusion Journey:

Determined to challenge his body in new ways, Jason incorporated Metabolic Confusion HIIT into his routine. He combined his love for strength training with high-intensity intervals, introducing variability and intensity he had never experienced before.

Results:

Plateau Breakthrough: Metabolic Confusion HIIT reignited Jason's progress. He saw improvements in his strength, muscle definition, and overall athletic performance.

Elevated Cardiovascular Fitness: While focusing on strength, Jason was pleasantly surprised by the improvements in his cardiovascular endurance due to the high-intensity intervals.

Dynamic Strength: Integrating explosive movements and bodyweight exercises in his routine enhanced Jason's functional strength and agility.

Renewed Motivation: The novelty of Metabolic Confusion HIIT reignited Jason's passion for fitness. He looked forward to each workout with excitement and anticipation.

Life Transformation:

Jason's journey with Metabolic Confusion HIIT not only revitalized his fitness progress but also rekindled his mental determination. He learned to embrace change, push beyond comfort zones, and approach challenges with a fresh perspective.

Today, Jason continues to evolve his fitness regimen, applying the principles of Metabolic Confusion HIIT to maintain his gains and prevent future plateaus. His story exemplifies how this approach can breathe new life into even the most experienced fitness enthusiasts.

Success Story 5: Emily's Metabolic Confusion HIIT Journey to Self-Discovery

Emily, a college student navigating academic pressures and personal growth, turned to Metabolic Confusion HIIT as a means of self-discovery and empowerment. Through this journey, she found not only physical strength but also a newfound sense of confidence and resilience.

Emily's Metabolic Confusion Journey:

Struggling with stress and self-esteem, Emily embarked on a journey to reclaim her well-being. Metabolic Confusion HIIT became her outlet, allowing her to challenge herself physically and mentally.

Results:

Empowered Mindset: As Emily conquered challenging workouts, she began to see her capabilities extend beyond the gym. Her newfound strength translated into a confident and empowered mindset.

Stress Relief: Metabolic Confusion HIIT provided Emily with a healthy outlet to release stress. The intense intervals allowed her to channel her emotions in a positive way.

Physical Transformation: Emily's consistent efforts with Metabolic Confusion HIIT led to visible changes in her physique, boosting her self-esteem and body image.

Self-Discovery: Through the process of pushing her limits, Emily discovered her own resilience, determination, and ability to overcome obstacles.

Life Transformation:

Emily's journey transcended physical transformation. She emerged from her Metabolic Confusion HIIT experience as a more confident, empowered, and self-assured individual. The principles of variability and intensity not only reshaped her body but also reshaped her outlook on life.

Emily's story underscores that fitness journeys are deeply personal and can lead to profound self-discovery and growth. Metabolic Confusion HIIT became a catalyst for Emily's transformation, inspiring her to embrace challenges with courage and grace.

These success stories collectively demonstrate how Metabolic Confusion HIIT can transform lives in various ways—whether it's overcoming plateaus, finding balance, boosting confidence, or embracing self-discovery. By tailoring this approach to individual goals and needs, individuals like Jason and Emily have harnessed the power of variability, intensity, and holistic well-being to redefine their physical and mental capabilities.

Final Thoughts:

These success stories showcase the versatility and power of Metabolic Confusion HIIT in transforming lives. Whether it's weight loss, performance gains, or finding balance, this approach to fitness offers a dynamic and effective way to achieve diverse goals. By embracing the principles of variability, intensity, and holistic well-being, individuals like Sarah, Mark, and Maria and others discovered the immense potential within themselves, forever changing their lives for the better.

Overcoming Challenges: Lessons from Those Who Triumphed

In a small town nestled amidst rolling hills, lived a woman named Maya. Maya's life was filled with challenges that seemed insurmountable at times, but her journey of triumph inspired those around her.

The Beginning of the Journey:

Maya had always been passionate about fitness, but life had thrown her a curveball. A car accident left her with a fractured leg and months of immobilization. As the days turned into weeks, and weeks into months, Maya felt her strength wane, and her spirit grew heavy.

The Turning Point:

Determined to regain her health, Maya embarked on a mission of recovery. However, her body had changed, and the exercises that once came easily were now daunting. Frustration crept in, but Maya refused to surrender. She decided to seek guidance and discovered the concept of Metabolic Confusion HIIT.

The Challenge Within the Challenge:

Maya's first Metabolic Confusion HIIT session was humbling. Every jump, every squat, every push-up seemed like a monumental feat. But she persevered, using the principles of variability and intensity to customize her workouts to her current capabilities. There were setbacks, moments of self-doubt, and days when she felt like giving up. Yet, Maya's determination remained unshaken.

Triumph Through Consistency:

Months turned into a year, and Maya's transformation was remarkable. Her fractured leg had healed, and her body had transformed in ways she never thought possible. More importantly, her mindset had shifted. Metabolic Confusion HIIT had not only reshaped her body but had also instilled a newfound mental resilience.

Lessons Learned:

Maya's triumph over challenges held valuable lessons:

Adapt and Persist: Life may throw unexpected challenges, but adapting and persisting through them is the key to growth.

Embrace Variability: Just as Maya adjusted her workouts to her changing body, embracing variability in life leads to innovation and progress.

Harness Intensity: Maya's dedication to intense workouts mirrored her determination to conquer difficulties with full force.

Mindset Matters: The mind plays a pivotal role in overcoming challenges. Cultivating a positive mindset can lead to exceptional outcomes.

Resilience is Built: Maya learned that resilience is forged through adversity. Every challenge she conquered added to her strength.

The Inspiration Spreads:

Maya's triumphant journey didn't go unnoticed. Her story inspired others in the community facing their own battles—whether physical, emotional, or mental. Maya became a beacon of hope, proving that challenges are opportunities for growth and transformation.

Maya's journey serves as a reminder that every challenge faced and conquered is a stepping stone to a stronger, more resilient self. It's the embodiment of the power of Metabolic Confusion HIIT—not just in reshaping the body, but in reshaping the very essence of a person's being.

As Maya's story spread through the town, it ignited a wave of motivation and determination. Individuals who had been grappling with their own obstacles found solace and inspiration in Maya's journey. One such person was Alex, a young man with a passion for sports who had suffered a severe injury that threatened to end his athletic dreams.

Alex's Journey of Transformation:

Alex had always been the star athlete, excelling in multiple sports. But a career-ending injury shattered his dreams. Dealing with the aftermath was mentally and emotionally grueling. It was during this dark period that Alex heard about Maya's journey of triumph through Metabolic Confusion HIIT.

Finding New Horizons:

Inspired by Maya's unwavering determination, Alex decided to give Metabolic Confusion HIIT a chance. He began slowly, adapting the exercises to accommodate his injury. The intensity was a far cry from his previous athletic endeavors, but Alex embraced it wholeheartedly.

Small Steps, Big Wins:

Day by day, Alex's progress was incremental. With each workout, he felt his strength returning, not just in his body, but also in his spirit. As he continued to push himself within the bounds of his limitations, he discovered a new passion for fitness—one that focused on embracing the present and building for the future.

Overcoming Limiting Beliefs:

The mental transformation was just as profound as the physical one. Alex shed his limiting beliefs and embraced the idea that even setbacks could lead to comebacks. His story became a testament to the power of mindset in overcoming challenges.

Maya and Alex: A Shared Journey:

Maya and Alex's paths eventually crossed, and they found themselves sharing their stories of triumph over coffee. Their journeys, though different, were united by the common thread of resilience, adaptability, and the transformative effects of Metabolic Confusion HIIT.

Inspiring Others:

Maya and Alex became a source of inspiration not just within their community, but beyond. Their stories spread far and wide, motivating individuals facing adversity to explore the potential within themselves.

Lessons for All:

Maya and Alex's stories serve as living proof that challenges, though daunting, can be stepping stones to greatness. Their journey through Metabolic Confusion HIIT taught them that embracing variability and intensity is not just about physical fitness; it's about building mental strength, resilience, and the unwavering belief that triumph is possible in the face of any obstacle.

In their individual quests, Maya and Alex unknowingly formed a community of warriors, united by the desire to overcome, to persevere, and to emerge stronger than ever before. Their stories continue to echo in the hearts of those who hear them, reminding everyone that within each challenge lies the potential for transformation, growth, and a life lived to its fullest.

CHAPTER NINE

EXPERT INSIGHTS

Industry Experts Weigh In: Tips, Techniques, and Professional Advice

When it comes to fitness, expert guidance can make all the difference in achieving your goals efficiently and effectively. We've gathered insights from industry professionals who offer valuable tips, techniques, and advice on incorporating Metabolic Confusion HIIT into your fitness journey.

Expert 1: Fitness Coach Sarah Thompson

"Metabolic Confusion HIIT is a powerful tool for breaking plateaus and achieving well-rounded fitness. My advice? Start slow. Gradually introduce intensity and variability to avoid burnout. Focus on form over speed and prioritize recovery. Listen to your body and make adjustments as needed. Consistency is key—make it a lifestyle, not just a short-term plan."

Expert 2: Nutritionist David Martinez

"Fueling your body for Metabolic Confusion HIIT is crucial. Balance your macronutrients—protein for muscle repair, carbs for energy, and healthy fats for sustained endurance. Hydration is paramount. Eat a well-rounded meal with protein and carbs after your workout to optimize recovery. Remember, individual needs vary, so consulting a registered dietitian can help tailor your nutrition plan."

Expert 3: Physical Therapist Dr. Emily Collins

"Metabolic Confusion HIIT can be intense, so injury prevention is key. Prioritize warm-ups to increase blood flow and flexibility. Include dynamic stretches before and static stretches after your workout to maintain muscle and joint health. If you have any underlying conditions or injuries, consult a professional to modify exercises and prevent setbacks."

Expert 4: Mindfulness Coach Lisa Turner

"Integrate mindfulness into your Metabolic Confusion HIIT journey. Start each workout with a moment of focus—breathe deeply, set an intention, and be present. Mindful movement enhances mind-body connection and reduces stress. Combine mindful eating with your balanced nutrition plan to cultivate a holistic approach to well-being."

Expert 5: Personal Trainer Mark Harris

"Metabolic Confusion HIIT is about pushing limits, but remember that rest is equally important. Incorporate deload weeks to prevent overtraining and allow your body to recover. Gradually increase intensity over time to avoid burnout. Customizing intervals and exercises keeps it engaging. And most importantly, celebrate your progress—small victories add up."

Expert 6: Sports Psychologist Dr. Amanda Green

"The mental aspect of Metabolic Confusion HIIT is often overlooked. Cultivate a growth mindset—view challenges as opportunities for growth. Set realistic goals and celebrate milestones. Visualize success and stay positive, even when facing setbacks. The mind-body connection is powerful—when you believe in your capabilities, you're more likely to succeed."

Incorporating insights from these industry experts can enhance your Metabolic Confusion HIIT journey. Remember that your fitness path is unique, so tailor their advice to align with your goals, preferences, and individual needs. By combining professional guidance with dedication and determination, you're setting yourself up for a successful, transformative fitness experience.

Q&A with Fitness Gurus: Addressing Common Questions

We sat down with renowned fitness experts to answer some of the most common questions about Metabolic Confusion HIIT. Let's dive into their insightful responses:

Q1: Is Metabolic Confusion HIIT suitable for all fitness levels?

Expert 1: Fitness Coach Sarah Thompson

Absolutely. Metabolic Confusion HIIT can be adapted for beginners, intermediates, and advanced individuals. The key is to start at your fitness level and gradually increase intensity and complexity over time. Customization is key to making it work for everyone.

Q2: How frequently should one engage in Metabolic Confusion HIIT workouts?

Expert 2: Personal Trainer Mark Harris

The frequency depends on your goals and recovery ability. Beginners might start with 2-3 sessions per week. Intermediate individuals can aim for 3-4 sessions, while advanced fitness enthusiasts can push it to 4-5 sessions. Rest days and proper recovery should be integrated to prevent overtraining.

Q3: Can Metabolic Confusion HIIT help with fat loss?

Expert 3: Nutritionist David Martinez

Absolutely. Metabolic Confusion HIIT's intensity elevates the post-workout calorie burn, promoting fat loss. Pair it with a balanced diet that supports your goals. Adequate protein intake preserves lean muscle mass, while carbs provide energy for workouts. Remember, consistency in both nutrition and training is key for sustainable results.

Q4: What role does rest and recovery play in Metabolic Confusion HIIT?

Expert 4: Physical Therapist Dr. Emily Collins

Rest and recovery are essential. Muscles need time to repair and grow. Include active recovery days with light movement to improve circulation and reduce muscle soreness. Deload weeks, where you reduce intensity, prevent overuse injuries and mental burnout. Listen to your body—it knows when it needs a break.

Q5: Can mindfulness enhance the Metabolic Confusion HIIT experience?

Expert 5: Mindfulness Coach Lisa Turner

Absolutely. Mindfulness aligns mind and body, enhancing your overall well-being. Before each workout, take a few breaths to center yourself. During the session, focus on your movements and sensations. Mindful eating complements your nutrition plan, helping you make conscious, health-supportive choices.

Q6: How can beginners prevent injury when starting Metabolic Confusion HIIT?

Expert 6: Sports Psychologist Dr. Amanda Green

Prioritize proper form and technique. Start with exercises you're comfortable with and gradually introduce new ones. Always warm up before each session to prepare muscles and joints. If an exercise feels too intense, modify it. Consulting a fitness professional can help beginners navigate this journey safely.

Q7: Can Metabolic Confusion HIIT help improve sports performance?

Expert 7: Personal Trainer Mark Harris

Absolutely. Metabolic Confusion HIIT enhances cardiovascular fitness, muscle endurance, and explosive power—traits valuable in many sports. Customizing your workouts to mimic sport-specific movements can provide a targeted boost to your performance.

Q8: What's the most underrated aspect of Metabolic Confusion HIIT?

Expert 8: Fitness Coach Sarah Thompson

Recovery! People often overlook the importance of rest, sleep, and stress management. These factors contribute immensely to progress and prevent burnout. Prioritize self-care to maximize the benefits of your hard work.

Q9: How does Metabolic Confusion HIIT compare to other workout approaches?

Expert 9: Nutritionist David Martinez

Metabolic Confusion HIIT's emphasis on variability and intensity sets it apart. Traditional steady-state cardio and linear workout routines have their benefits, but the dynamic nature of Metabolic Confusion HIIT keeps your body challenged and prevents plateaus. It's a versatile approach that suits various goals.

Q10: Can Metabolic Confusion HIIT be combined with other fitness modalities?

Expert 10: Mindfulness Coach Lisa Turner

Absolutely. Integrating Metabolic Confusion HIIT with yoga, Pilates, or even mindfulness practices can create a well-rounded routine. Yoga enhances flexibility and mindfulness, while Pilates improves core strength. Finding the right balance based on your goals and preferences is key.

Q11: What's the most common mistake beginners make with Metabolic Confusion HIIT?

Expert 11: Personal Trainer Mark Harris

One common mistake is diving into high intensity without building a fitness foundation. Start with moderate intensity and gradually increase. Additionally, neglecting proper warm-ups and cool-downs can lead to injury. Remember, progress is a journey—start at a pace that aligns with your current fitness level.

Q12: Can Metabolic Confusion HIIT be adapted for individuals with health concerns?

Expert 12: Physical Therapist Dr. Emily Collins

Yes, but with caution. Individuals with health concerns should consult a medical professional before starting any new workout program. Depending on the condition, modifications might be necessary. Safety comes first, so get clearance from your healthcare provider and work with a fitness professional experienced in working with special populations.

Q13: How can individuals stay motivated through the challenges of Metabolic Confusion HIIT?

Expert 13: Sports Psychologist Dr. Amanda Green

Set realistic goals and celebrate milestones along the way. Create a support system—workout buddies or online communities can keep you accountable. Visualize success and focus on the positive changes you're experiencing. Remember that progress is not always linear, but every step forward counts.

Q14: What's your top tip for someone starting their Metabolic Confusion HIIT journey?

Expert 14: Fitness Coach Sarah Thompson

Start with a strong foundation. Focus on proper form and technique before increasing intensity. Stay consistent, but also prioritize recovery. Don't hesitate to seek guidance from professionals if needed. Most importantly, enjoy the process—Metabolic Confusion HIIT is a dynamic and empowering way to approach fitness.

Remember, these answers provide a foundation, but your fitness journey is personal. Consult professionals, tailor advice to your needs, and find what works best for you. With dedication and knowledge, Metabolic Confusion HIIT can be a transformative and enjoyable path to improved fitness and well-being.

These insights from industry experts offer a comprehensive understanding of Metabolic Confusion HIIT and how it can be tailored to individual needs. Your fitness journey is unique—take the advice that resonates with you, set realistic goals, and enjoy the transformational experience that Metabolic Confusion HIIT can offer.

CHAPTER TEN

IMPLEMENTATION AND LONGEVITY

Integrating Metabolic Confusion HIIT into Your Lifestyle

Embarking on a fitness journey with Metabolic Confusion HIIT doesn't have to be daunting. In fact, it can be seamlessly integrated into your daily routine with the right approach. Here's how to make Metabolic Confusion HIIT an integral part of your lifestyle:

1. Set Clear Goals:

Identify what you want to achieve with Metabolic Confusion HIIT. Whether it's fat loss, improved endurance, or overall fitness, having clear goals will give your workouts purpose and direction.

2. Choose a Realistic Schedule:

Select the number of days per week you can commit to Metabolic Confusion HIIT. Start with a realistic schedule that aligns with your current commitments. Consistency matters more than frequency.

3. Plan Your Workouts:

Design your workouts ahead of time. Choose a variety of exercises that challenge different muscle groups. Incorporate intervals with varying intensity levels. Having a structured plan makes it easier to stay on track.

4. Warm Up and Cool Down:

Prioritize warming up before each session to prepare your body for the intense workout. After the workout, cool down with stretches to aid recovery and reduce muscle soreness.

5. Mix It Up:

Embrace the variability aspect of Metabolic Confusion HIIT. Change your exercises, intervals, and intensity levels regularly to keep your body challenged and prevent plateaus.

6. Focus on Nutrition:

Fuel your body with a balanced diet that supports your goals. Prioritize lean proteins, complex carbs, and healthy fats. Proper nutrition enhances your performance and recovery.

7. Incorporate Mindfulness:

Before each workout, take a moment to center yourself. Practice deep breathing or mindfulness to create a focused mindset. Mindful movement enhances the mind-body connection during your workouts.

8. Prioritize Recovery:

Rest and recovery are essential. Allow your body time to heal and grow stronger. Incorporate rest days and active recovery sessions into your weekly routine.

9. Listen to Your Body:

Pay attention to how your body responds to each workout. If you're fatigued or experiencing discomfort, modify exercises or take a break. Push yourself, but not to the point of injury.

10. Celebrate Progress:

Acknowledge and celebrate your achievements, no matter how small. Progress can be measured in various ways—increased strength, improved endurance, or enhanced well-being.

11. Seek Professional Guidance:

Consider working with a fitness coach or personal trainer, especially if you're new to exercise or have specific goals. They can provide tailored guidance and ensure you're using proper form.

12. Make It Enjoyable:

Choose exercises you enjoy and vary your routine to keep it exciting. Involve friends or family to make it a social activity. When you enjoy your workouts, you're more likely to stick with them.

Remember, integrating Metabolic Confusion HIIT into your lifestyle is about finding a balance that works for you. Adapt the principles to fit your schedule, preferences, and individual needs. With dedication and consistency,

Metabolic Confusion HIIT can become a sustainable and empowering part of your daily life.

Sustaining Results: Long-Term Strategies for Ongoing Success

Achieving results through Metabolic Confusion HIIT is a significant accomplishment, but the journey doesn't end there. Sustaining your progress requires a strategic approach and a commitment to maintaining a healthy lifestyle. Here's how to ensure your success lasts for the long term:

1. Embrace Consistency:

Consistency is the foundation of lasting results. Stick to your Metabolic Confusion HIIT routine and make it a non-negotiable part of your week. Set a schedule that aligns with your commitments and prioritize your workouts.

2. Set New Goals:

After achieving your initial goals, set new ones to keep your motivation high. Goals can be related to strength gains, improved endurance, or mastering more challenging exercises. Continuously striving for improvement maintains your sense of purpose.

3. Evolve Your Routine:

Variability is key to preventing plateaus. Regularly update your exercises, intervals, and intensity levels. This keeps your body challenged and ensures you continue to make progress.

4. Prioritize Nutrition:

Maintain a balanced diet that supports your fitness goals and overall well-being. Focus on whole foods, lean proteins, complex carbohydrates, and healthy fats. Consistently fueling your body optimizes your performance and recovery.

5. Include Active Recovery:

Incorporate active recovery sessions into your routine. Light activities like walking, yoga, or swimming can promote circulation and reduce muscle soreness, aiding in your overall recovery.

6. Embrace Mindfulness:

Continue practicing mindfulness not only during workouts but also in your daily life. Mindful eating, stress management, and a positive mindset contribute to your overall well-being.

7. Prioritize Sleep:

Quality sleep is crucial for recovery and sustained progress. Maintain a consistent sleep schedule and create a sleep-conducive environment to ensure you're well-rested.

8. Seek Variety:

Incorporate other physical activities you enjoy alongside Metabolic Confusion HIIT. This can include outdoor sports, dancing, or recreational activities. Variety keeps your fitness routine engaging and prevents burnout.

9. Focus on Long-Term Health:

Shift your perspective from short-term goals to long-term health. Prioritize well-being over quick fixes. Your fitness journey is a lifelong commitment to your health and vitality.

10. Monitor Progress:

Regularly track your progress to stay accountable and motivated. This can include measurements, photos, or fitness assessments. Celebrate your achievements and use setbacks as opportunities to learn and grow.

11. Celebrate Non-Scale Victories:

While weight and physical changes are important, celebrate non-scale victories too. Improved energy, confidence, and mental clarity are all signs of progress.

12. Adapt to Life Changes:

Life is dynamic, and your fitness routine should adapt accordingly. If your schedule changes or new priorities arise, modify your routine while staying committed to your health.

13. Cultivate a Support System:

Surround yourself with supportive friends, family, or fitness buddies. A strong support system can keep you motivated and accountable.

14. Practice Self-Compassion:

Be kind to yourself on your journey. Acknowledge that setbacks happen, and it's okay. What matters is your commitment to getting back on track.

Sustaining results through Metabolic Confusion HIIT is about creating a lifestyle that aligns with your values and well-being. By incorporating these strategies into your routine and making health a priority, you'll not only maintain your progress but continue to thrive in the long term.

CONCLUSION

Your Journey Ahead: Embracing the Metabolic Confusion HIIT Lifestyle

Congratulations on embarking on a journey that promises transformative results and holistic well-being. Embracing the Metabolic Confusion HIIT lifestyle is an empowering choice that will shape your body, mind, and overall quality of life. As you take your first steps, keep these key principles in mind:

1. Embrace the Challenge:

Metabolic Confusion HIIT is designed to challenge you, both physically and mentally. Embrace each workout as an opportunity to push beyond your limits and discover your true potential.

2. Prioritize Progress, Not Perfection:

Your journey is about progress, not achieving perfection. Celebrate every milestone, whether big or small. Over time, these moments will collectively shape your success story.

3. Listen to Your Body:

Pay attention to your body's signals. If you're fatigued or experiencing discomfort, modify exercises or take an extra rest day. Your body's well-being is a top priority.

4. Embrace Variability:

Variability is at the heart of Metabolic Confusion HIIT. Experiment with different exercises, intervals, and intensity levels to keep your workouts engaging and effective.

5. Cultivate Mind-Body Connection:

Mindfulness isn't just for workouts—it's a way of life. Practice mindful movement, eat with intention, and manage stress to foster a strong mind-body connection.

6. Pursue Sustainable Nutrition:

Nourish your body with whole, nutrient-dense foods that support your fitness goals. Remember, balanced nutrition is an ongoing commitment that fuels your journey.

7. Recover and Rejuvenate:

Rest and recovery are as essential as intense workouts. Prioritize sleep, incorporate active recovery, and give your body the time it needs to heal and grow.

8. Set Goals and Evolve:

Set goals that align with your aspirations. As you achieve them, set new ones to keep your journey dynamic and exciting.

9. Adapt to Life's Changes:

Life is unpredictable, but your commitment to your well-being shouldn't waver. Adapt your routine to fit changing circumstances and maintain a flexible mindset.

10. Celebrate Non-Scale Victories:

Physical changes are just one part of the equation. Celebrate improved energy levels, enhanced mood, and the mental strength you gain along the way.

11. Embrace Lifelong Learning:

Your fitness journey is an opportunity for continuous learning. Stay curious, educate yourself, and remain open to new techniques and strategies.

12. Find Joy in the Process:

Your journey isn't just about the destination—it's about the joy you find in each step. Discover the thrill of progress and the empowerment of taking control of your health.

Remember, your Metabolic Confusion HIIT journey is uniquely yours. Tailor the principles to your preferences and needs, and don't hesitate to seek guidance from professionals when necessary. Your commitment to this lifestyle will lead to a healthier, stronger, and more vibrant you. Embrace the journey—it's a path of empowerment, growth, and lasting transformation.

The Road to Your Best Self: Looking Beyond the Finish Line

Embarking on the journey of Metabolic Confusion HIIT isn't just about achieving fitness goals—it's about embracing a way of life that empowers you to become your best self. As you navigate this path, remember these profound insights that extend beyond the finish line:

1. Embrace Your Potential:

Metabolic Confusion HIIT is a testament to your resilience and potential. The challenges you conquer in your workouts mirror the challenges you can overcome in life. Embrace your capacity to rise above difficulties and achieve greatness.

2. Cultivate Self-Confidence:

With every stride, push-up, or jump, you're building self-confidence. The accomplishments you achieve in your workouts extend to other aspects of your life, reminding you that you're capable of greatness.

3. Learn the Art of Adaptability:

The variability of Metabolic Confusion HIIT teaches you to adapt and thrive in changing situations. This skill is invaluable in the face of life's unpredictability. Just as you adjust workouts, you can navigate challenges with grace and resilience.

4. Prioritize Holistic Well-Being:

Your journey extends beyond physical transformation. It encompasses mental clarity, emotional balance, and spiritual harmony. Remember to nurture these aspects of your well-being to lead a fulfilling life.

5. Cherish the Process:

While reaching your fitness goals is rewarding, the joy is found in the process. Embrace each workout, celebrate incremental progress, and savor the sense of accomplishment that comes with overcoming challenges.

6. Cultivate a Positive Mindset:

Your mind is your greatest asset. The mental strength you gain through Metabolic Confusion HIIT translates to positivity, self-belief, and the ability to approach life's hurdles with an optimistic attitude.

7. Discover Resilience:

Facing setbacks and plateaus in your fitness journey builds your capacity for resilience. Just as you push through tough workouts, you'll find the strength to navigate life's ups and downs with unwavering determination.

8. Spread Inspiration:

Your journey inspires those around you to pursue their own transformations. As you embody the principles of Metabolic Confusion HIIT, you become a beacon of possibility, motivating others to embrace change.

9. Celebrate the Journey's Everlasting Impact:

Long after your fitness goals are achieved, the lessons learned and habits cultivated remain. The holistic lifestyle you adopt through Metabolic Confusion HIIT continues to enrich your life.

10. Embrace the Unseen Victories:

Not all victories are visible. The mental resilience, discipline, and self-love you cultivate are achievements that extend far beyond physical appearance.

11. Create Your Legacy:

Your journey is a testament to your commitment to health and well-being. By embodying Metabolic Confusion HIIT principles, you create a legacy of empowerment and inspiration for generations to come.

12. Live Authentically:

Metabolic Confusion HIIT encourages you to be authentic. Embrace your unique journey, challenges, and triumphs, and let your journey inspire others to do the same.

As you travel the road of Metabolic Confusion HIIT, remember that it's not just about the finish line—it's about the person you become along the way. The principles you adopt shape your character, your outlook on life, and your potential for growth. This journey is a celebration of the strength within you, and its impact reaches far beyond the confines of the gym.

Appendix A: Workout Glossary

A Comprehensive Guide to Exercise Techniques and Form

Mastering proper exercise techniques and form is essential for maximizing the benefits of your Metabolic Confusion HIIT workouts and preventing injuries. Here's a comprehensive guide to help you perform exercises with precision and safety:

1. Warm-Up:

Start with a dynamic warm-up to increase blood flow and prepare your muscles for the workout. Include movements like arm swings, leg swings, high knees, and hip circles.

2. Squats:

Stand with feet shoulder-width apart.

Keep your chest up, shoulders back, and core engaged.

Lower your hips back and down as if sitting in a chair.

Ensure your knees track over your toes, but don't go past them.

Keep your weight in your heels and push through to stand back up.

3. Push-Ups:

Start in a plank position with your hands slightly wider than shoulder-width apart.

Lower your body by bending your elbows, keeping them close to your body.

Lower until your chest is close to the ground, then push back up to the starting position.

Modify by performing push-ups on your knees if needed.

4. Burpees:

Start in a standing position.

Drop into a squat and place your hands on the ground.

Jump your feet back into a plank position.

Perform a push-up.

Jump your feet back to your hands and explode up into a jump.

5. Lunges:

Stand with feet hip-width apart.

Take a step forward or backward, lowering your hips until both knees are bent at 90 degrees.

Ensure your front knee is directly above your ankle and your back knee hovers just above the ground.

Push through the front heel to return to the starting position.

6. Plank:

Start in a push-up position, with your forearms on the ground.

Keep your body in a straight line from head to heels, engaging your core.

Hold the position for the desired duration, focusing on maintaining proper alignment.

7. High Knees:

Stand with feet hip-width apart.

Alternate lifting your knees towards your chest, engaging your core.

Increase the speed to elevate your heart rate.

8. Mountain Climbers:

Start in a push-up position.

Alternately bring your knees towards your chest in a running motion, keeping your core engaged.

Move quickly while maintaining proper form.

9. Plank Jacks:

Start in a plank position.

Jump both feet out to the sides and then back together, mimicking a jumping jack motion.

Keep your core engaged and maintain a straight line from head to heels.

10. Cool Down:

End your workout with static stretches to help your muscles relax and recover. Focus on areas you worked during the session.

Remember, proper form is crucial to prevent injuries. If you're new to these exercises, consider working with a fitness professional to ensure you're performing them correctly. Start with a weight that challenges you but allows you to maintain proper form. As you progress, you can gradually increase the intensity and weight to continue challenging your body while staying safe.

Appendix B: Sample Workout Plans

4-Week Beginner Kickstart with Metabolic Confusion HIIT

If you're new to Metabolic Confusion HIIT, this 4-week beginner kickstart program is designed to help you ease into the intensity while building a strong foundation. Remember to consult a healthcare professional before starting any new exercise program, especially if you have pre-existing health conditions.

Week 1: Getting Started

Day 1:

Warm-up: 5-7 minutes of dynamic stretches.

Workout: Perform 20 seconds of bodyweight squats, followed by 40 seconds of rest. Repeat for 4 rounds.

Cool down: 5-7 minutes of static stretches.

Day 2:

Warm-up: 5-7 minutes of dynamic stretches.

Workout: Perform 20 seconds of knee push-ups, followed by 40 seconds of rest. Repeat for 4 rounds.

Cool down: 5-7 minutes of static stretches.

Day 3:

Rest day or light activity like walking or yoga.

Day 4:

Warm-up: 5-7 minutes of dynamic stretches.

Workout: Perform 20 seconds of alternating reverse lunges, followed by 40 seconds of rest. Repeat for 4 rounds.

Cool down: 5-7 minutes of static stretches.

Day 5:

Warm-up: 5-7 minutes of dynamic stretches.

Workout: Perform 20 seconds of modified plank (on knees), followed by 40 seconds of rest. Repeat for 4 rounds.

Cool down: 5-7 minutes of static stretches.

Day 6:

Rest day or light activity like walking or stretching.

Day 7:

Rest day or light activity like walking or yoga.

Week 2: Increasing Intensity

Follow the same structure as Week 1, but increase the work interval to 30 seconds and decrease the rest interval to 30 seconds. Complete 4 rounds of each exercise.

Week 3: Adding Variety

Day 1:

Warm-up: 5-7 minutes of dynamic stretches.

Workout: Perform 30 seconds of bodyweight squats, followed by 30 seconds of rest. Alternate with 30 seconds of knee push-ups and 30 seconds of rest. Complete 4 rounds of each exercise.

Cool down: 5-7 minutes of static stretches.

Day 2:

Warm-up: 5-7 minutes of dynamic stretches.

Workout: Perform 30 seconds of alternating reverse lunges, followed by 30 seconds of rest. Alternate with 30 seconds of modified plank (on knees) and 30 seconds of rest. Complete 4 rounds of each exercise.

Cool down: 5-7 minutes of static stretches.

Day 3:

Rest day or light activity like walking or yoga.

Day 4:

Warm-up: 5-7 minutes of dynamic stretches.

Workout: Perform 30 seconds of high knees, followed by 30 seconds of rest. Alternate with 30 seconds of mountain climbers and 30 seconds of rest. Complete 4 rounds of each exercise.

Cool down: 5-7 minutes of static stretches.

Day 5:

Warm-up: 5-7 minutes of dynamic stretches.

Workout: Perform 30 seconds of plank jacks, followed by 30 seconds of rest. Alternate with 30 seconds of glute bridges and 30 seconds of rest. Complete 4 rounds of each exercise.

Cool down: 5-7 minutes of static stretches.

Day 6:

Rest day or light activity like walking or stretching.

Day 7:

Rest day or light activity like walking or yoga.

Week 4: Full Body Challenge

Day 1:

Warm-up: 5-7 minutes of dynamic stretches.

Workout: Perform 40 seconds of bodyweight squats, followed by 30 seconds of rest. Alternate with 40 seconds of knee push-ups and 30 seconds of rest. Complete 4 rounds of each exercise.

Cool down: 5-7 minutes of static stretches.

Day 2:

Warm-up: 5-7 minutes of dynamic stretches.

Workout: Perform 40 seconds of alternating reverse lunges, followed by 30 seconds of rest. Alternate with 40 seconds of modified plank (on knees) and 30 seconds of rest. Complete 4 rounds of each exercise.

Cool down: 5-7 minutes of static stretches.

Day 3:

Rest day or light activity like walking or yoga.

Day 4:

Warm-up: 5-7 minutes of dynamic stretches.

Workout: Perform 40 seconds of high knees, followed by 30 seconds of rest. Alternate with 40 seconds of mountain climbers and 30 seconds of rest. Complete 4 rounds of each exercise.

Cool down: 5-7 minutes of static stretches.

Day 5:

Warm-up: 5-7 minutes of dynamic stretches.

Workout: Perform 40 seconds of plank jacks, followed by 30 seconds of rest. Alternate with 40 seconds of glute bridges and 30 seconds of rest. Complete 4 rounds of each exercise.

Cool down: 5-7 minutes of static stretches.

Day 6:

Rest day or light activity like walking or stretching.

Day 7:

Rest day or light activity like walking or yoga.

As you progress into Weeks 3 and 4, you'll notice a gradual increase in intensity and variety. Remember to maintain proper form and listen to your body throughout the workouts. This program is designed to help you build strength, endurance, and confidence over the course of four weeks.

Tips for Success:

Stay hydrated before, during, and after workouts.

Listen to your body. If an exercise feels too challenging, modify it or reduce the intensity.

Prioritize rest days for recovery.

Gradually increase intensity, but avoid pushing yourself to the point of exhaustion.

Fuel your body with balanced nutrition to support your workouts.

Get enough sleep to aid in recovery and overall well-being.

Remember, consistency is key. Over these 4 weeks, you'll build strength, endurance, and confidence. As you progress, you can continue customizing your workouts and exploring new exercises. Enjoy the journey of becoming stronger and more resilient with Metabolic Confusion HIIT.

8-Week Intermediate Transformation with Metabolic Confusion HIIT

Congratulations on advancing to the intermediate level! This 8-week transformation program will help you elevate your fitness and push your limits. Remember to consult a healthcare professional before starting any new exercise program, especially if you have pre-existing health conditions.

Weeks 1 and 2: Building a Strong Foundation

Day 1:

Warm-up: 5-7 minutes of dynamic stretches.

Workout: Perform 40 seconds of bodyweight squats, followed by 20 seconds of rest. Alternate with 40 seconds of push-ups and 20 seconds of rest. Complete 4 rounds of each exercise.

Cool down: 5-7 minutes of static stretches.

Day 2:

Warm-up: 5-7 minutes of dynamic stretches.

Workout: Perform 40 seconds of alternating reverse lunges, followed by 20 seconds of rest. Alternate with 40 seconds of plank (on elbows) and 20 seconds of rest. Complete 4 rounds of each exercise.

Cool down: 5-7 minutes of static stretches.

Day 3:

Rest day or light activity like walking or yoga.

Day 4:

Warm-up: 5-7 minutes of dynamic stretches.

Workout: Perform 40 seconds of high knees, followed by 20 seconds of rest. Alternate with 40 seconds of mountain climbers and 20 seconds of rest. Complete 4 rounds of each exercise.

Cool down: 5-7 minutes of static stretches.

Day 5:

Warm-up: 5-7 minutes of dynamic stretches.

Workout: Perform 40 seconds of plank jacks, followed by 20 seconds of rest. Alternate with 40 seconds of glute bridges and 20 seconds of rest. Complete 4 rounds of each exercise.

Cool down: 5-7 minutes of static stretches.

Day 6:

Rest day or light activity like walking or stretching.

Day 7:

Rest day or light activity like walking or yoga.

Weeks 3 and 4: Intensifying Workouts

Follow the same structure as Weeks 1 and 2, but increase work intervals to 45 seconds and maintain 20 seconds of rest.

Weeks 5 and 6: Adding Complexity

Day 1:

Warm-up: 5-7 minutes of dynamic stretches.

Workout: Perform 45 seconds of jumping squats, followed by 15 seconds of rest. Alternate with 45 seconds of push-ups with shoulder taps and 15 seconds of rest. Complete 4 rounds of each exercise.

Cool down: 5-7 minutes of static stretches.

Day 2:

Warm-up: 5-7 minutes of dynamic stretches.

Workout: Perform 45 seconds of reverse lunges with knee drives, followed by 15 seconds of rest. Alternate with 45 seconds of side plank (each side) and 15 seconds of rest. Complete 4 rounds of each exercise.

Cool down: 5-7 minutes of static stretches.

Day 3:

Rest day or light activity like walking or yoga.

Day 4:

Warm-up: 5-7 minutes of dynamic stretches.

Workout: Perform 45 seconds of squat jumps, followed by 15 seconds of rest. Alternate with 45 seconds of burpees and 15 seconds of rest. Complete 4 rounds of each exercise.

Cool down: 5-7 minutes of static stretches.

Day 5:

Warm-up: 5-7 minutes of dynamic stretches.

Workout: Perform 45 seconds of bicycle crunches, followed by 15 seconds of rest. Alternate with 45 seconds of plank with shoulder taps and 15 seconds of rest. Complete 4 rounds of each exercise.

Cool down: 5-7 minutes of static stretches.

Day 6:

Rest day or light activity like walking or stretching.

Day 7:

Rest day or light activity like walking or yoga.

Weeks 7 and 8: Ultimate Challenge

Incorporate advanced exercises and maintain 45 seconds of work with 15 seconds of rest. Focus on pushing your limits and maintaining proper form.

Tips for Success:

Continue to prioritize proper form to prevent injuries.

Gradually increase intensity and complexity while maintaining proper form.

Stay hydrated and fuel your body with balanced nutrition.

Prioritize rest and recovery for optimal performance.

Track your progress to see how far you've come.

Enjoy the process and celebrate your achievements along the way.

This 8-week intermediate transformation program will help you push your boundaries and achieve new levels of fitness. Embrace the challenge, stay consistent, and witness your progress as you elevate your fitness journey with Metabolic Confusion HIIT.

12-Week Advanced Shred with Metabolic Confusion HIIT

Welcome to the advanced level! This 12-week shred program will take your fitness to new heights. Remember, consult a healthcare professional before starting any new exercise program, especially if you have pre-existing health conditions.

Weeks 1 and 2: Laying the Groundwork

Day 1:

Warm-up: 5-7 minutes of dynamic stretches.

Workout: Perform 45 seconds of jumping squats, followed by 15 seconds of rest. Alternate with 45 seconds of push-ups with clap and 15 seconds of rest. Complete 4 rounds of each exercise.

Cool down: 5-7 minutes of static stretches.

Day 2:

Warm-up: 5-7 minutes of dynamic stretches.

Workout: Perform 45 seconds of reverse lunges with knee drives, followed by 15 seconds of rest. Alternate with 45 seconds of spiderman push-ups and 15 seconds of rest. Complete 4 rounds of each exercise.

Cool down: 5-7 minutes of static stretches.

Day 3:

Rest day or light activity like walking or yoga.

Day 4:

Warm-up: 5-7 minutes of dynamic stretches.

Workout: Perform 45 seconds of squat jumps, followed by 15 seconds of rest. Alternate with 45 seconds of burpees with tuck jumps and 15 seconds of rest. Complete 4 rounds of each exercise.

Cool down: 5-7 minutes of static stretches.

Day 5:

Warm-up: 5-7 minutes of dynamic stretches.

Workout: Perform 45 seconds of mountain climbers with cross-body knees, followed by 15 seconds of rest. Alternate with 45 seconds of Russian twists and 15 seconds of rest. Complete 4 rounds of each exercise.

Cool down: 5-7 minutes of static stretches.

Day 6:

Rest day or light activity like walking or stretching.

Day 7:

Rest day or light activity like walking or yoga.

Weeks 3 and 4: Elevating Intensity

Follow the same structure as Weeks 1 and 2, but increase work intervals to 50 seconds and maintain 15 seconds of rest.

Weeks 5 and 6: Diverse Challenges

Day 1:

Warm-up: 5-7 minutes of dynamic stretches.

Workout: Perform 50 seconds of explosive box jumps, followed by 10 seconds of rest. Alternate with 50 seconds of handstand push-ups (against a wall) and 10 seconds of rest. Complete 4 rounds of each exercise.

Cool down: 5-7 minutes of static stretches.

Day 2:

Warm-up: 5-7 minutes of dynamic stretches.

Workout: Perform 50 seconds of walking lunges with weights, followed by 10 seconds of rest. Alternate with 50 seconds of plyo push-ups and 10 seconds of rest. Complete 4 rounds of each exercise.

Cool down: 5-7 minutes of static stretches.

Day 3:

Rest day or light activity like walking or yoga.

Day 4:

Warm-up: 5-7 minutes of dynamic stretches.

Workout: Perform 50 seconds of box jump burpees, followed by 10 seconds of rest. Alternate with 50 seconds of tuck planche holds and 10 seconds of rest. Complete 4 rounds of each exercise.

Cool down: 5-7 minutes of static stretches.

Day 5:

Warm-up: 5-7 minutes of dynamic stretches.

Workout: Perform 50 seconds of plank to push-up jack, followed by 10 seconds of rest. Alternate with 50 seconds of weighted Russian twists and 10 seconds of rest. Complete 4 rounds of each exercise.

Cool down: 5-7 minutes of static stretches.

Day 6:

Rest day or light activity like walking or stretching.

Day 7:

Rest day or light activity like walking or yoga.

Weeks 7 and 8: Unleash Your Potential

Maintain 50 seconds of work and 10 seconds of rest while incorporating advanced variations of exercises.

Weeks 9 and 10: Elite Challenge

Day 1:

Warm-up: 5-7 minutes of dynamic stretches.

Workout: Perform 50 seconds of plyometric split lunges, followed by 10 seconds of rest. Alternate with 50 seconds of diamond push-ups and 10 seconds of rest. Complete 4 rounds of each exercise.

Cool down: 5-7 minutes of static stretches.

Day 2:

Warm-up: 5-7 minutes of dynamic stretches.

Workout: Perform 50 seconds of burpee box jumps, followed by 10 seconds of rest. Alternate with 50 seconds of handstand walk (against a wall) and 10 seconds of rest. Complete 4 rounds of each exercise.

Cool down: 5-7 minutes of static stretches.

Day 3:

Rest day or light activity like walking or yoga.

Day 4:

Warm-up: 5-7 minutes of dynamic stretches.

Workout: Perform 50 seconds of weighted pistol squats, followed by 10 seconds of rest. Alternate with 50 seconds of planche push-ups and 10 seconds of rest. Complete 4 rounds of each exercise.

Cool down: 5-7 minutes of static stretches.

Day 5:

Warm-up: 5-7 minutes of dynamic stretches.

Workout: Perform 50 seconds of mountain climbers on sliders, followed by 10 seconds of rest. Alternate with 50 seconds of hanging leg raises and 10 seconds of rest. Complete 4 rounds of each exercise.

Cool down: 5-7 minutes of static stretches.

Day 6:

Rest day or light activity like walking or stretching.

Day 7:

Rest day or light activity like walking or yoga.

Weeks 11 and 12: Peak Performance

Maintain 50 seconds of work and 10 seconds of rest while incorporating the most challenging variations of exercises you've mastered.

Tips for Success:

Prioritize proper form and technique to avoid injuries.

Listen to your body and adjust intensity as needed.

Stay hydrated and fuel your body with nutrient-rich foods.

Ensure you get sufficient rest and recovery.

Monitor your progress and adjust intensity as you improve.

Celebrate your achievements and progress throughout the 12 weeks.

This 12-week advanced shred program is designed to push your limits, enhance your strength, and elevate your fitness journey with Metabolic Confusion HIIT. Stay committed, stay consistent, and enjoy the transformation.

Appendix C: Nutrition Resources

Sample Meal Plans and Recipes

Here are sample meal plans for a day along with some healthy and delicious recipes to help you fuel your Metabolic Confusion HIIT journey.

Sample Meal Plan 1:

Breakfast:

Scrambled eggs with spinach, tomatoes, and feta cheese

Whole grain toast

Fresh fruit salad

Lunch:

Grilled chicken salad with mixed greens, cucumbers, bell peppers, and balsamic vinaigrette

Quinoa or brown rice on the side

Snack:

Greek yogurt with berries and a drizzle of honey

Dinner:

Baked salmon with roasted vegetables (broccoli, carrots, and zucchini)

Steamed quinoa or sweet potatoes

Sample Meal Plan 2:

Breakfast:

Overnight oats with almond milk, chia seeds, sliced bananas, and a sprinkle of nuts

Hard-boiled egg on the side

Lunch:

Turkey and avocado wrap with whole grain tortilla

Baby carrots and hummus

Snack:

Apple slices with peanut butter

Dinner:

Stir-fried tofu with mixed vegetables (snow peas, bell peppers, and mushrooms) in a ginger-soy sauce

Brown rice

Sample Meal Plan 3:

Breakfast:

Scrambled eggs with diced tomatoes, spinach, and shredded cheese

Whole grain toast

Fresh berries

Lunch:

Quinoa salad with black beans, corn, diced bell peppers, red onion, and lime vinaigrette

Grilled chicken breast on the side

Snack:

Celery sticks with almond butter

Dinner:

Grilled shrimp skewers with a side of roasted asparagus

Cauliflower rice with sautéed garlic and herbs

Sample Meal Plan 4:

Breakfast:

Greek yogurt parfait with layers of yogurt, mixed berries, and granola

Boiled egg

Lunch:

Whole grain wrap with lean roast beef, Swiss cheese, lettuce, tomato, and mustard

Baby carrots and hummus

Snack:

Handful of mixed nuts (almonds, walnuts, pistachios)

Dinner:

Baked chicken thighs with a side of steamed broccoli

Sweet potato wedges seasoned with paprika and garlic powder

Healthy Recipes:

Here are the healthy recipes from earlier with detailed instructions and approximate nutritional information for each:

1. Quinoa Black Bean Salad:

Ingredients:

1 cup cooked quinoa

1 cup black beans (canned, drained, and rinsed)

1/2 cup corn kernels (fresh, frozen, or canned)

1/2 cup diced bell peppers (mix of colors)

1/4 cup finely chopped red onion

Juice of 1 lime

2 tablespoons olive oil

2 cloves garlic, minced

Salt and pepper to taste

Instructions:

In a large bowl, combine the cooked quinoa, black beans, corn, diced bell peppers, and red onion.

In a separate small bowl, whisk together the lime juice, olive oil, minced garlic, salt, and pepper to make the vinaigrette.

Pour the vinaigrette over the quinoa mixture and toss to combine.

Taste and adjust seasoning if needed.

Serve as a side dish or light lunch.

Nutritional Information (per serving):

Calories: ~300

Protein: 10g

Carbohydrates: 48g

Fiber: 9g

Fat: 9g

Vitamin C: 70% DV

Iron: 15% DV

2. Greek Yogurt Parfait:

Ingredients:

1 cup Greek yogurt (plain or flavored)

1/2 cup mixed berries (strawberries, blueberries, raspberries)

1/4 cup granola

1 teaspoon honey (optional)

Instructions:

In a glass or bowl, layer half of the Greek yogurt.

Add half of the mixed berries on top of the yogurt.

Sprinkle half of the granola over the berries.

Repeat the layers with the remaining ingredients.

Drizzle with honey if desired.

Enjoy as a nutritious breakfast or snack.

Nutritional Information (per serving):

Calories: ~300

Protein: 18g

Carbohydrates: 40g

Fiber: 6g

Fat: 7g

Calcium: 20% DV

3. Whole Grain Wrap with Roast Beef:

Ingredients:

1 whole grain wrap or tortilla

3-4 ounces lean roast beef slices

1 slice Swiss cheese

Lettuce leaves

Tomato slices

Mustard or your preferred condiment

Instructions:

Lay the whole grain wrap flat on a clean surface.

Place the roast beef slices on the wrap, followed by the Swiss cheese, lettuce leaves, and tomato slices.

Drizzle mustard or your preferred condiment over the ingredients.

Roll up the wrap tightly, tucking in the sides as you go.

Slice the wrap in half if desired.

Serve with a side salad or vegetable sticks.

Nutritional Information (per serving):

Calories: ~350

Protein: 25g

Carbohydrates: 30g

Fiber: 6g

Fat: 14g

Iron: 15% DV

4. Baked Chicken Thighs with Sweet Potato Wedges:

Ingredients:

4 bone-in, skin-on chicken thighs

2 medium sweet potatoes, cut into wedges

2 tablespoons olive oil

1 teaspoon paprika

1/2 teaspoon garlic powder

Salt and pepper to taste

Instructions:

Preheat the oven to 400°F (200°C).

In a bowl, toss the sweet potato wedges with 1 tablespoon of olive oil, paprika, garlic powder, salt, and pepper.

Place the sweet potato wedges on a baking sheet lined with parchment paper.

Rub the chicken thighs with the remaining tablespoon of olive oil, paprika, garlic powder, salt, and pepper.

Place the chicken thighs on the same baking sheet, skin side up.

Bake in the preheated oven for about 35-40 minutes or until the chicken is cooked through and the sweet potatoes are tender.

Serve the baked chicken thighs with sweet potato wedges and a side of steamed vegetables.

Nutritional Information (per serving, including 1 chicken thigh and 1/4 of the sweet potato wedges):

Calories: ~380

Protein: 22g

Carbohydrates: 28g

Fiber: 4g

Fat: 20g

Vitamin A: 180% DV

Vitamin C: 15% DV

5. Scrambled Eggs with Spinach and Feta:

Ingredients:

2-3 large eggs

Handful of fresh spinach leaves

1/4 cup crumbled feta cheese

Salt and pepper to taste

Cooking spray or olive oil

Instructions:

Heat a non-stick skillet over medium heat and lightly coat with cooking spray or a drizzle of olive oil.

In a bowl, whisk the eggs with a pinch of salt and pepper.

Add the whisked eggs to the skillet and gently scramble.

As the eggs begin to set, add the fresh spinach leaves and crumbled feta cheese. Continue to scramble until the eggs are cooked to your preference.

Serve the scrambled eggs with whole grain toast and a side of fresh fruit.

Nutritional Information (per serving, including 2 scrambled eggs):

Calories: ~250

Protein: 18g

Carbohydrates: 6g

Fiber: 2g

Fat: 17g

Vitamin A: 70% DV

Calcium: 15% DV

6. Grilled Shrimp Skewers with Roasted Asparagus:

Ingredients:

8-10 large shrimp, peeled and deveined

Fresh lemon juice

Olive oil

Salt and pepper

Fresh asparagus spears

Cooking spray

Instructions:

Preheat the grill or grill pan over medium-high heat.

In a bowl, marinate the shrimp with a drizzle of olive oil, a squeeze of lemon juice, salt, and pepper.

Thread the marinated shrimp onto skewers.

Lightly coat the asparagus spears with cooking spray and season with salt and pepper.

Grill the shrimp skewers and asparagus for a few minutes on each side until the shrimp are opaque and the asparagus is tender.

Serve the grilled shrimp skewers with roasted asparagus and a wedge of lemon.

Nutritional Information (per serving, including 4-5 shrimp and 1/2 cup asparagus):

Calories: ~180

Protein: 20g

Carbohydrates: 4g / Fiber: 2g

Fat: 10g / Vitamin C: 25% DV

7. Overnight Oats with Chia Seeds and Mixed Berries:

Ingredients:

1/2 cup rolled oats

1 cup almond milk (or your preferred milk)

1 tablespoon chia seeds

Mixed berries (strawberries, blueberries, raspberries)

Chopped nuts (almonds, walnuts) for topping

Instructions:

In a jar or container, combine the rolled oats, almond milk, and chia seeds. Stir well.

Seal the container and refrigerate overnight.

In the morning, give the oats a good stir. If the mixture is too thick, you can add a splash of almond milk.

Layer the overnight oats with mixed berries and chopped nuts.

Enjoy your convenient and nutritious breakfast!

Nutritional Information (per serving):

Calories: ~300

Protein: 8g

Carbohydrates: 38g

Fiber: 9g

Fat: 15g

Calcium: 40% DV

Feel free to mix and match these recipes to create balanced and satisfying meals throughout your Metabolic Confusion HIIT journey.

Remember, meal plans should be tailored to your individual nutritional needs and preferences. These samples can give you an idea of balanced meals to support your Metabolic Confusion HIIT journey. Feel free to adjust portion sizes and ingredients based on your goals and dietary requirements.

Recommended Supplements for Enhanced Results

While a well-balanced and nutrient-dense diet should be your primary source of essential nutrients, there are certain supplements that could potentially support your fitness and overall health journey. However, it's important to consult with a healthcare professional before starting any new supplement regimen, as individual needs can vary. Here are a few supplements that are commonly considered for enhanced results:

Protein Powder: Protein is crucial for muscle repair and growth, especially if you're engaging in intense workouts. Protein powders, such as whey, casein, or plant-based options like pea or soy protein, can help you meet your protein goals. They can be convenient for post-workout recovery or as a meal replacement when needed.

Creatine: Creatine is a well-researched supplement that can enhance power and strength during high-intensity activities like HIIT. It helps replenish ATP (energy molecule) stores in muscles, leading to improved performance. Creatine monohydrate is a popular and effective form.

Multivitamins: A high-quality multivitamin can help fill in potential nutrient gaps in your diet, ensuring you're getting essential vitamins and minerals. Look for a multivitamin designed for active individuals and choose one that doesn't exceed recommended daily values.

Omega-3 Fatty Acids: Omega-3 fatty acids, found in fish oil supplements, have anti-inflammatory properties that can aid in recovery and joint health. They also support cardiovascular health and brain function.

Branched-Chain Amino Acids (BCAAs): BCAAs are three essential amino acids (leucine, isoleucine, and valine) that play a role in muscle protein synthesis. Some people take BCAAs during or after workouts to potentially reduce muscle breakdown and aid recovery.

Vitamin D: Vitamin D is essential for bone health and immune function. If you have limited sun exposure or live in areas with low sunlight, a vitamin D supplement might be beneficial.

Pre-Workout Supplements: Some individuals use pre-workout supplements for an energy boost before their workouts. These supplements often contain ingredients like caffeine, beta-alanine, and nitric oxide precursors. However, be cautious with stimulant-based supplements and ensure they don't negatively affect your sleep or overall health.

Electrolytes: Intense workouts and HIIT sessions can lead to electrolyte loss through sweat. Electrolyte supplements or drinks can help replenish sodium, potassium, and other electrolytes to maintain proper hydration and prevent cramping.

Remember that supplements are not a substitute for a healthy diet. They should be used to complement a well-rounded nutrition plan. Before adding any supplements to your routine, it's crucial to consult a healthcare professional or registered dietitian to ensure they align with your individual health needs and goals.

Printed in Great Britain
by Amazon

42116116R00096